# Catalogue of Pictures in the Posession of Beriah Botfield, Esq. at Norton Hall

*From the Author*

# CATALOGUE

OF

# PICTURES

IN THE POSSESSION OF

# BERIAH BOTFIELD, ESQ.

AT

## NORTON HALL.

LONDON:

1848.

LONDON  WILLIAM NICOL, 60, PALL MALL

# PREFACE.

THE present Collection has been formed with the sole intention of adding to the comforts of an English home the additional luxury of " walls hung round with thoughts."

This Catalogue has been printed with the view of preserving those minute particulars, which, if not recorded at the time, are lost for ever. Much that seems trivial to us may be interesting to our descendants, and property of whatever kind is not the less valuable because it may be associated with its traditions.

Elaborate descriptions are but imperfect vehicles for conveying ideas of pictorial representations. No language, however glowing, can paint with sufficient distinctness the impressions conveyed to the mind by the best works of the Old Masters. All should be said which is necessary for the identification of the Painting, but beyond this the busy power of the imagination may be happily substituted for any force of words.

Whenever the Paintings are on any other material than canvass, the fact has been noticed, and the figures annexed to each denote the heighth and width of the frame, shewing the space occupied by the Picture on the wall.

The Dictionaries of Painters by Bryan, Pilkington and Ticozzi have furnished the dates affixed to the name of each Artist. Copies of known pictures are entered under the name of the original master.

The names assigned to each picture are those under which they came into my possession.

B. B.

*Norton Hall, Sept.* 1, 1848.

# CATALOGUE

OF

# PICTURES.

---

## A. AGLIO.

London 1811.

## T. STOTHARD.

Born 1755.  Died 1834.

View of Jerusalem from the Garden of Olives, the Figures by Stothard.  From the Collection of Mr. Harwood.  Height, 7 feet, 2 inches.  Width, 10 feet, 2 inches.

## ANTONISSEN.

Pupil of Ommeganck.

D. 1826.

Landscape with Cattle — Morning.  On Panel.  H. 2 ft. 6 in.  W. 3 ft.

Landscape with Cattle — Evening.  On Panel.  H. 2 ft. 6 in.  W. 3 ft.

From the Collection of Sir Felix Agar.

## JACQUES D'ARTOIS.

B. at Brussels 1613   D there 1665.

## DAVID TENIERS, JUN.

B. at Antwerp 1610   D at Brussels 1694

A Village Fête, the Landscape by Artois, the Figures by
Teniers. From the Collection of James Gibbs, Esq.  H. 4 ft.
6 in.  W. 5 ft. 6 in.

## PETER JOHN VAN ASCH.

B at Delft 1603.

View near Haerlem; with his Monogram.  Imported from
Holland.  On Panel.  H. 2 ft. 4 in.  W. 2 ft. 11 in.

## JOHN ASSELYN.

B at Antwerp 1610   D. 1660.

View of Ponte Rotto on the Tiber at Rome.  From the
Collection of Count Pourtales at Paris, and J. Rogers, Esq.,
London.  H. 2 ft. 6 in.  W. 2 ft. 10 in.

## GIACOMO BAHTIA.

Bastia 1753.

View of the Ruins of the Palace of the Cæsars at Rome;
signed " Gio. Bahtia, Bastia, 1753."  Purchased at Christie's.
H. 2 ft. 5½ in.  W. 2 ft. 11 in.

## FEDERIGO BAROCCIO.

B. at Urbino 1528.   D 1612

The Holy Family reposing under a tree in the Wilderness.
From the Collection of Monsieur le Comte Michel at Paris,
1846.  On Copper.  H. 1 ft. 8½ in.  W. 1 ft. 6½ in.

The Virgin and Child receiving the Adoration of a Monk, presented by an Angel; St. Joseph and the Ass standing by. H. 2 ft. 1 in. W. 1 ft. 9 in.

## GIACOMO DA PONTE, IL BASSANO.
### B. at Bassano 1510. D. there 1592

A Pastoral Scene with Cattle and Figures. Imported from Paris, 1846. H. 2 ft. 4 in. W. 2 ft. 9 in.

## J. BASSI.
### Rome.

## DESSOULAVY.

View of the Alban Grotto, and Lake of Albano, with Figures by Dessoulavy, 1845. H. 2 ft. 3 in. W. 1 ft. 11 in.

## ABRAHAM BEGEYN.
### B. 1650. D. circa 1710

Peasants with Cattle, near some ruins. An Italian Landscape after the manner of Berghem. From the Collection of the Chevalier Cousin at Paris, 1846. On Panel. H. 1 ft. 11 in. W. 1 ft. 9 in.

## WILLIAM BENNETT.
### Woodstock.

Portrait of a Black Mare. H. 2 ft. 8 in. W. 3 ft. 6 in.

Portrait of a Bay Mare. H. 2 ft. 8 in. W. 3 ft. 6 in.
Two favourite hunters of Beriah Botfield at Oxford, in 1824-8.

Fox breaking Cover. H. 2 ft. W. 2 ft. 3½ in.

## NICHOLAS BERGHEM.

### B at Haerlem 1624    D. there 1683

Landscape with Figures, &c.   A Church tower in the distance.   From the Collection of Wynne Ellis, Esq.   H. 4 ft. 9 in.   W. 6 ft.

## GERARD BERKHEYDEN.

### B. at Haerlem 1645.   D. there 1693.

View of the Stadt House at Haerlem.   From the Collection of Mr. Mc Lellan of Glasgow.   H. 4 ft. 10. in.   W. 6 ft. 4 in.

View of the Entrance to a town in the Low Countries, with Figures; a Gentleman on horseback, followed by a man driving Cows home in the Evening.   From the Collection of the Rev. C. Digby.   H. 2 ft.   W. 2 ft. 3 in.

## HENRY JOHN BODDINGTON.

### Fulham

South East View of Norton Hall, Northamptonshire, taken from the Deer Park, shewing the Garden Front of the Mansion; signed " H. J. B. 1848."   H. 3 ft. 1 in.   W. 4 ft. 2 in.

North East View of Norton Hall, shewing the Entrance Front and the Village Church, as seen from Coneygree; signed " H. J. B. 1848."   H. 3 ft. 1 in.   W. 4 ft. 2 in.

South East View of Norton Hall, with the Terrace Garden, taken from the Park; signed " H. J. B. 1848."   H. 3 ft. 5 in.   W. 3 ft.

## CHARLES BLAAR.
### Rome.

The Bride of Genzano; with that town in the distance.
H. 3 ft. 10 in.   W. 3 ft. 2 in.

## JOHN FRANCIS VAN BLOEMEN, ORIZZONTE.
### B. at Antwerp 1656.   Died at Rome 1740.

Landscape, a woody scene.   H. 3 ft. 5 in.   W. 4 ft. 4 in.

Landscape, on a river.   H. 3 ft. 5 in.   W. 4 ft. 4 in.
From the Collection of Mr. Palmer at Kingston.

## PETER BLOOT.
### D. 1667

A Village Scene in Flanders, with Peasants regaling them-
selves before an Alehouse.   H. 2 ft. 2½ in.   W. 2 ft. 11 in.

## J. BODEMAN.
### Holland 1847.

View on the borders of the Rhine, with a Chateau on the
opposite bank of the river, a Passage Boat with Cattle and
Persons crossing; signed " Bodeman ft. 1846." Purchased
from the Artist, who painted it during his stay in London.
H. 2 ft. 1 in.   W. 2 ft. 6 in.

## BOILLY.
### Paris c. 1792.

### A Pair of Interiors.
The Forget Me Not.   H. 2 ft. 6½ in.   W. 2 ft. 3 in.

The Miniature.   H. 2 ft. 6½ in.   W. 2 ft. 3 in.
In the Costume of the French Revolution.   Imported from
Paris, 1845.

## FERDINAND BOL.

B at Dort 1612. D. there 1681.

Portrait of a Burgomaster, æt. 30, dated 1633. From the Collection of P. Huggett, Esq. of Sandgate, near Ramsgate. H. 4 ft. 5 in. W. 3 ft. 3 in.

Portrait of Admiral Van Tromp, signed and dated 1664. From the Collection of Mr. Abbott. H. 4 ft. 4 in. W. 3 ft. 7 in.

## BONIFAZIO VENEZIANO.

B at Venice 1491. D. there 1563.

The Holy Family, St. Joseph and St. John the Baptist, with St. Catherine, Santa Lucia and another Saint offering Homage to the Virgin and Infant Jesus. From the Collection of Count Barba at Ferrara. H. 5 ft. 6 in. W. 6 ft. 6 in.

## JACQUES COURTOIS, IL BORGOGNONE.

B 1621. D. 1676.

A Battle Piece. From the Collection of the Duke of Lucca, 1841. H. 2 ft. 8 in. W. 3 ft. 2 in.

## JOHN BOTH.

B at Utrecht 1610. D there 1650.

A Rocky Landscape, under sunshine. Italian Peasants in the foreground; signed " J. Both." From the Collection of Count Bernardi, late Procureur du Roi, Charles X., at Bordeaux. H. 2. ft. 6½ in. W. 2 ft. 1½ in.

## JOHN BOTH.

## NICHOLAS BERGHEM.

### B. Haerlem 1624.   D. 1683.

Landscape on the banks of the Tiber by John Both, the Figures by Berghem   From Manchester.  H. 5 ft. 6 in. W. 6 ft. 6 in.


## FRANCIS BOUCHER.

### B. at Paris 1704.   D. there 1770

A Lady with a Book.  Imported from Paris.  H. 5 ft. 2 in. W. 4 ft. 2 in.


## J. BOULTBEE.

### Leicester.

The Dun Horse, called the Shropshire Poney, ridden by Beriah Botfield in Leicestershire, taken July 28, 1803.

" Picture of a favourite Hunting Horse by Lord Clive's Arabian, nearly fifteen hands high, 22 years old last spring, the property of Beriah Botfield, has been in his possession since he was four years old and hunted every season and never was beat.   He went a Fox Chace in Leicestershire, with Mr. Meynell's hounds in November 1799, of 55 minutes with a very large field of horses, and himself and two more were the only horses in at the death of the Fox, from which he got the title of the Shropshire Poney.  This picture was taken Dec. 1st 1799, by Mr. Boultbee, but not being a good likeness he painted him again July 28, 1803, when he painted the grey horse, and mare at Ditton.   He was bred by Lord Powis and bought by Thomas Botfield at three years old for Eleven Guineas and a half from a man who lived at a place called Ness Cliff between Shrewsbury and Oswestry.

T. Botfield wishing to part with him B. Botfield requested his Mother to buy him which she did for Twenty Guineas, and presented the horse to him." H. 1 ft. 11 in. W. 2 ft. 5½ in.

Portrait of a favourite Hackney Grey Mare, called Frisky, 16 years old, the property of Beriah Botfield, Esq. with his old servant, Edward Nicholls, and a favourite Spaniel Dog, called Bustle, painted July 28, 1803. H. 2 ft. 6 in. W. 3 ft.

Portrait of Crazy, a favourite Mare bred by Beriah Botfield, Esq. who hunted with her in 1802, &c. H. 2 ft. 6 in. W. 3 ft.

Portrait of a Grey Horse, ridden by Thomas Botfield of Dawley, and of John Darroll, his Groom, who died in Beriah Botfield's service at Norton Hall. H. 2 ft.6 in. W. 3 ft.

### SEBASTIAN BOURDON.
#### B at Montpellier 1616. D. at Paris 1671.

Holy Family, the Infant Saviour and St. John, with the Virgin and St. Joseph reposing in Egypt. From the Collection of Baron Buckmann at Ghent. H. 3 ft. 6½ in. W. 4 ft 8½ in.

### RAINIER BRAKENBURG.
#### B at Haerlem 1649.

Peasants merry-making before a Dutch Village Alehouse, bearing the sign of the Thirsty Stag. From the Collection of William Rickford Collett, Esq., 1844. H. 2 ft. 10 in. W. 3 ft. 1 in.

## C. BROOKING.

### B at Deptford c 1720, D. 1759.

A Sea Piece, with a Man of War firing a Salute, off a Coast. From the Collection of the Countess of Mansfield on Richmond Hill. Cat. p. 34, No. 36, June 1844, signed " C. Brooking." H. 2 ft. ½ in. W. 2 ft. 8 in.

## F. CALVERT.

Buttevant Abbey, Cork. H. 1 ft 8 in. W. 2 ft. 1½ in.

Lochland Castle, Perthshire. H. 1 ft. 8 in. W. 2 ft. 1½ in.

1829. Cork Harbour. H. 2 ft. 2 in. W. 2 ft. 9 in.

1830. Liverpool. H. 2 ft. 3 in. W. 2 ft 10 in.

## CANGEZA.

### DRAWING MASTER, HARROW.

1822. View of Harrow on the Hill. H. 7½ in. W. 9½ in.

## ANNIBALE CARACCI.

### B at Bologna 1560. D. at Rome 1609.

Virgin and Infant Jesus with St. John, a repetition of the subject known as " La Vierge au Voile," by the divine Raffaelle in the Louvre. From the Collection of John Theobald, Esq. H. 3 ft. 4 in. W. 2 ft. 10 in.

## ANTONIO CARACCI, IL GOBBO.

### B. at Venice 1583  D. at Rome 1618.

Virgin and Child. H. 4 ft. 1 in. W. 3 ft. 4 in.

## MICHEL ANGELO AMERIGI DA CARAVAGGIO.

B at Caravaggio 1569.    D at Porto Ercole 1609.

The Entombment of Christ.    An early copy of the masterpiece of this great master, formerly in the Chiesa Nuova at Rome, whence it was removed to the Louvre, and restored to the Vatican at Rome.    The present copy was imported from Italy, and was for some time the chief ornament of the Picture Gallery at Daventry.    H. 12 ft.    W. 8 ft. 11 in.

## GIOVANNI BENEDETTO CASTIGLIONE.

B. at Genoa 1616.    D at Mantua 1670.

Madonna and Bambino.    Purchased at Christie's.    H. 4 ft. 4½in.    W. 3 ft. 6 in.

## GIACOMO CAVEDONE.

B at Sassuolo 1577.    D at Bologna 1660

Susannah and the Elders.    From the Collection of Sir Simon Clarke, Bart.    H. 6 ft. 1 in.    W. 7 ft. 5 in.

## LUDOVICO CARDI, CIGOLI.

B at Cigoli 1559.    D at Florence 1613

Christ in the Garden of Olives.    From the Collection of Prince Paul of Wirtemberg.    H. 2 ft. 4 in.    W. 2 ft.

## ALFRED CLINT.

London.

View of Hastings and the East Cliff, from the Sands—Hazy Morning.    Exhibited among the Works of British Artists in Suffolk Street, 1844.    H. 2 ft. 2 in.    W. 2 ft. 10¾ in.

## CHARLES COLEMAN.

### Rome.

Buffalo Cart and Peasants of the Pontine Marshes on the Road from Rome to Naples; signed " C. Coleman, Roma, 1845." H. 3 ft. 8 in. W. 4 ft. 7 in.

Buffaloes in their natural state on the Pontine Marshes, the Circœan Promontory in the distance; signed " C. Coleman, Roma, 1845." H. 3 ft. 8 in. W. 4 ft. 7 in.

Buffalo Cart with Italian Peasants; Harvest in the Pontine Marshes; signed " C. Coleman, Roma, 1846." II. 5 ft. 6 in. W. 7 ft.

Driving Buffaloes in the Pontine Marshes; clearing the streams from weeds, &c.; signed " C. Coleman, Roma, 1847."

" The subject of it [the picture] is the manner in which they make use of Buffaloes to trample down and clear the rivers and canals of the tall rank weeds, which choke up the streams, causing them to overflow and by that means producing mal-aria. The scene in nature is very animated, for although the animals are half amphibious, and consequently very fond of the water, they are particularly averse to be driven against their wills, and also against the stream up to their chins in the water, sometimes wading, sometimes swimming, goaded on by men armed with long poles, who follow close after them in a flat shallow boat, called a sandola, and not being very merciful to the poor animals, they find it rather fatiguing work, and consequently are for ever trying to make their escape up the bank, which is always prevented by men placed on each side of the stream, some on horseback, which renders any attempt on the part of the poor buffaloes of making an exit quite hopeless. The animation of the scene in nature is of course very much enhanced by the shouting of

the men, the prancing of their horses, the plunging and snort-
ing of the buffaloes in the water, and the flight of the
affrighted birds which fly off in all directions." H. 5 ft. 6 in.
W. 7 ft.

## LIEUTENANT CONDÉ.

### The Devonshire Wilkie.

#### Plymouth

Interior of a Devonshire Cottage — Peasants' Repast.
H. 2 ft. 4 in. W. 2 ft. 8 in.

## ANTONIO ALLEGRI, CORREGGIO.

#### B. at Parma 1490 D. there 1534.

Cleopatra dissolving the Pearl; with the Artist's Monogram.
Imported from Spain. H. 5 ft. 7 in. W. 5 ft.

## POMPONIO ALLEGRI, CORREGGIO.

#### B at Parma 1522.

The Holy Family. Formerly the altar-piece of the private
chapel of the Sanvitali family at Parma; presented by them
to the Benedictine Convent in that city. The archives date
the donation soon after the death of the painter. Purchased
from G. Bryant Lane at Rome in 1845. H. 3 ft. 6 in.
W. 3 ft.

## SAMUEL COX.

#### Daventry.

Portrait of Turpin, a Grey Pony of B. Botfield's. H. 2 ft.
7 in. W. 3 ft.

Portrait of Multum, a Black Pony of do. II. 3 ft. W. 3 ft. 6 in.

Portrait of Spider, a Bay Pony, and Dogs of do. II. 3 ft. 3 in. W. 4 ft.

Portrait of Lion, a Newfoundland Dog, and Juba, a Pug Dog of Mrs. Botfield's, in the north front of Norton Hall. H. 3 ft. 6 in  W. 4 ft. 9 in.

View of Norton Hall in 1829, from the Watling Street. H. 2 ft. 7 in.  W. 3 ft. 5 in.

View of Daventry from Bonyl Hill. H. 2 ft. 7 in. W. 3 ft. 5 in.

## DANIEL CUNLIFFE.
### London
Fox Hounds in Cover.  Obtained from the Artist. II. 2 ft. 7 in.  W. 3 ft. 1 in.

## JEREMIAH DAVISON.
### B 1695.  D 1745.
Portrait of Kitty Clive, the celebrated actress.  From the Collection of Horace Walpole at Strawberry Hill, to whom it was presented by her brother, Mr. James Raftor. Cat. p. 208.  H. 5 ft. 3 in.  W. 4 ft. 3 in.

## GEORGE DAWE.
### A. R. A. 1810.  D. in London 1829.
Portrait of the Duke of Cumberland, subsequently the King of Hanover, 1812.  Engraved by W. Sams, from whom it was purchased.  H. 3 ft. 11 in.  W. 3 ft. 2 in.

## FRANCIS DECKER.

### Holland c. 1650.

Avenue of Trees, with Figures, and a Cottage, Mecklenburg in the distance; signed "Decker ft." From the Mecklenburg Collection. On Panel. H. 2 ft. 10 in. W. 2 ft. 7 in.

## ABRAHAM VAN DIEPENBECK.

### B. at Bois le Duc 1607. D. at Antwerp 1675.

The Holy Family. From the Collection of Mr. Fripp of Bristol. On Panel. H. 2 ft. 7 in. W. 3 ft. 1 in.

## CHRISTIAN WILLIAM ERNEST DIETRICK.

### B. at Weimar 1712 D at Dresden 1774.

View of the Cascatelli at Tivoli; signed "Dietrick, 1758." From the Collection of the Chevalier Cousin at Paris, 1846. H. 2 ft. 7 in. W. 3 ft. 3 in.

## AGNESE DOLCI.

### DAUGHTER OF CARLO DOLCI.

### B. at Florence c. 1650.

Portrait of Santa Cecilia at her instrument. From the Collection of M. Ricardi at Florence. H. 4 ft. 6 in. W. 3 ft. 9 in.

Portrait of St. Clothilde of France bearing the Oriflamme of St. Denis. From the Collection of the Chevalier Cousin at Paris, 1846. H. 3 ft. 2½ in. W. 2 ft. 8 in.

St. Agnes. From a Church at Leghorn, since demolished. H. 4 ft. 5 in. W. 3 ft. 7 in.

## CARLO DOLCI.

### B. at Florence 1616.  D. 1686.

The Madonna in a blue robe, a reduced copy made in 1827, from the original at Blenheim, by THOMAS AUSTIN. On Panel.  H. 1 ft. 11 in.  W. 1 ft. 8½ in.

## DOMENICHINO, DOMENICO ZAMPIERI.

### B. at Bologna 1581   D. at Naples 1641.

Ceres. From the Collection of Mr. John Attwood. H. 5 ft. 9 in.  W. 5 ft. 3 in.

## JOHN LE DUC.

### B at The Hague 1636   D there 1695.

The Spoils of War — Cavaliers regaling.  On Panel. H. 2 ft. 5 in.  W. 3 ft. 3 in.

## GERBRANT VANDER EECKHOUT.

### B at Amsterdam 1621.  D there 1674.

The Presentation in the Temple.  From the Collection of Mr. Baxter at Manchester.  H. 5 ft. 3 in.  W. 6 ft. 6 in.

## ALDRET VAN EVERDINGEN.

### B at Alkmaar 1621.  D 1675.

Landscape in the Low Countries.  Imported from Holland.  H. 3 ft. 8 in.  W. 4 ft 6 in.

## JOHN BAPTIST FRANCK.

### B at Antwerp 1600

Interior of a Picture Gallery, which the Proprietor is exhibiting to his friends.  From the Collection of Herr J. Kleinenbergh, M. D. of Leyden, more than 80 years a Collector of Pictures at that place, sold 19th July, 1841. Cat. Lot 42. On Panel. H. 3 ft. W. 3 ft. 8 in.

## FREDERICK FRANKS.

### B. in England. D. at Rome 1843.

View of the Church of St. Giorgio in Velabro, the only Church in Rome dedicated to the tutelary Saint of England, and the Arch of Septimius Severus, taken from the Arch of Janus Quadrifrons in the Velabrum, near the Forum at Rome. H. 2 ft. 6½ in. W. 2 ft. 1½ in.

## THOMAS GAINSBOROUGH.

### B. 1727. D. in London 1788.

Landscape, with Market Cart and Figures proceeding along a rural lane leading to a Common, on the left are some red tiled buildings, on the right a hedge-row. In the distance appears the Church tower of Henny in Suffolk, the Birth-place of the Artist; one of his early productions. From Mr. Lake's Collection. H. 2 ft. 8 in. W. 3 ft. ½ in.

## BENVENUTO TISIO, GAROFALO.

### B. at Ferrara 1481. D 1559

The Holy Family, seated, in a Landscape, with buildings, &c. From the Collection of Monsieur Ferriere Laffitte at Paris, 1846. H. 2 ft. 7 in. W. 2 ft. 2 in.

## LUCA GIORDANO.

### B. at Naples 1632. D. there 1705

Holy Family. The Virgin and St. Joseph, with the Infant Jesus. Imported from Italy, 1847. H. 3 ft. 9 in. W. 3 ft. 5 in.

## JOHN GLOVER.

View of Harrow on the Hill, from Lord Northwick's Park, with the Mansion of that Nobleman, for whom it was painted at a charge of 100 Guineas, and from whom it was purchased. No. 17 in his Catalogue of Modern Pictures. H. 4 ft. 10 in. W. 4 ft. 3 in.

Landscape, a Composition, with Ruins, and Cattle. H. 3 ft. W. 4 ft.

## JOHN VAN GOYEN.

### B. at Leyden 1596. D at the Hague 1656.

View on a River in Holland, with Boats, &c. in a fresh breeze. Imported from Paris, 1844. II. 1 ft. 10 in. W. 2 ft. 5 in.

View near Leyden; signed with the date 1644. On Panel. H. 1 ft. 9 in. W. 2 ft. 3 in.

View on a river in Holland, with Fishermen dragging their nets; signed " V. Goyen." Imported from Paris, 1846. H. 2 ft. 3 in. W. 3 ft.

Landscape with Figures, a view of a town in Holland; signed " V. Goyen," dated 1642. Imported from Holland. On Panel. H. 1 ft. 8 in. W. 2 ft. 4 in.

## JOHN HACKAERT.

### B at Amsterdam 1636. D. 1699.

## JOHN LINGELBACH.

### B 1625. D. 1687

Italian Landscape on a river, with a Bridge, and distant Mountains, with Figures by John Lingelbach; signed " Hackaert." Imported from Paris, 1844. H. 3 ft. 5 in. W. 4 ft. 4 in.

## ADRIAN HANNEMANN.

B. at the Hague 1611.   D. 1680

Portrait of Sir Kenelm Digby; signed "Hannemann, A°. 1654." H. 3 ft. 4 in.   W. 2 ft. 9 in.

## GERARD VAN HARP.

PUPIL OF RUBENS.

The Infant Hercules. On Copper. H. 1 ft. 5 in. W. 1 ft. 8 in.

St. Bavon distributing Alms. Imported from Holland. On Copper. H. 3 ft. 6 in.   W. 4 ft. 4 in.

Esther before Ahasuerus. From the Collection of M. Schamp D'Aveschoot at Ghent. No. 83 in Catalogue. H. 3 ft. 3 in.   W. 4 ft.

Dutch Cabaret, Boors Regaling. An Interior with Card Players. From the Collection of W. D. Acraman, Esq. at Clifton. No. 198 in the Catalogue. On Copper. H. 3 ft. 4½in.   W. 4 ft. 2½ in.

The Infant Hercules. On Copper. H. 1 ft. 5 in. W. 1 in. 8 in.

## BARTHOLOMEW VAN DER HELST.

B. at Haerlem 1613.   D. at Amsterdam 1670.

Portrait of the Herr Dirk Van Collen; Lord of Bredelar, and Burgomaster. He resided at the Village of Petersburg near Amsterdam; signed " Van der Helst, 1657." From the Collection of M. Van Huten at Utrecht. H. 5 ft. W. 4 ft. 1 in.

## T. C. HOFLAND.

View of the Upper end of Loch Lomond—Evening.
From the Collection of the Earl of Coventry, in London.
H. 2 ft. 9 in.  W. 3 ft. 8 in.

## WILLIAM HOGARTH.

B in London 1697.  D. there 1764.

Portrait of Kitty Fisher.  H. 4 ft. 1 in.  W. 3 ft. 4 in.

## HOLME.

PUPIL OF SIR JOSHUA REYNOLDS.

London

Portrait of Laurence Sterne, Author of Tristram Shandy.
H. 5 ft. 5½in.  ·W. 4 ft. 8 in.

## T. L. HORNBROOK.

Portsmouth Harbour.  H. 2 ft. 10 in.  W. 3 ft. 9 in.

## JOHN VAN HUYSUM.

B. at Amsterdam 1682  D. there 1749.

Landscape with Ruins; signed " Jan Van Huysum."
From the Collection of Sir Thomas Baring.  H. 2 ft. 10 in.
W. 3 ft.

A Classical Landscape, representing the Worship of Bacchus; thus described in the Catalogue d'un Amateur, p. 10.
" Dans un riant paysage dix prêtresses de Bacchus viennent
offrir des présents à ce dieu; elles entourent sa statue, objet de
leur culte, et tandis qu'elles l'invoquent, et deposent leurs
offrandes à ses pieds, le vieux Silène, chancelant sur son âne,
s'est pris la main dans un guépier.  Des plantes de toutes

sortes, des fleurs, des broussailles, le gazon le plus verdoyant, décorent le premier plan; les lointains sont encore ornés par des villes bâties dans un charmant pays, derrière lequel des montagnes se pendent à l'horizon. Ce magnifique paysage, tres poetiquement composé, est clair dans toutes ses parties, d'une couleur transparente, et du fini le plus précieux auquel l'art puisse atteindre. Conservation parfaite." Signed, "Jan van Huysum fecit." From the Collection of Monsieur de Trucy. H. 3 ft. 1 in. W. 2 ft. 6 in.

### CORNELIUS JANSSEN.
#### B. at Amsterdam 1590. D 1665

Portrait of George Villiers, first Duke of Buckingham, the Minister of James, and Charles I.; signed " C. J. 1657." H. 1 ft. 3½ in. W. 1 ft. 2 in.

Portrait of Sir George Villiers, father of George, Duke of Buckingham. From Horace Walpole's Collection at Strawberry Hill. On Panel. Cat. p. 213. H. 4 ft. 6 in. W. 3 ft. 6 in.

Portrait of Prince Rupert; signed and dated, 1659. From the Collection of P. Huggett, Esq. of Sandgate. H. 4 ft. 10 in. W. 4 ft.

### ABRAHAM JANSSENS.
#### B. Antwerp 1569. D there 1631.

The Prodigal Son. Signed. H. 2 ft. W. 2 ft. 4 in.

Return of the Prodigal. H. 2 ft. W. 2 ft. 4 in.
#### On Copper.

## ANTONIO JOLI.

### B. at Modena 1700    D in 1777.

View of the City of Madrid. Signed on the back of the canvas, " Joli," with the date of 1750. H. 2 ft. 4½ in. W. 4 ft. 3 in.

## HARRIET KEARSLEY.

### London.

The Flower and the Leaf. From Chaucer; signed " H Kearsley." H. 2 ft. 5 in. W. 2 ft.

## WILLIAM DE KEISAR.

### B. at Antwerp 1647    D 1693.

Portrait of a Gentleman or Cotton Merchant of Holland, seated at a table. From the Collection of R. Simmons, Esq. H. 3 ft. W. 2 ft. 4½ in.

## SIR GODFREY KNELLER.

### B at Lubeck 1648    D. at London 1723.

Portrait of the Duchess of Cleveland; signed and dated 1684. H. 4 ft. 9 in. W. 4 ft.

## SOLOMON KONINCK.

### B at Amsterdam 1609.

A Dutch Philosopher and his Family, being the portrait of Cornelius De Hooft, the translator of Homer into Dutch; a favourite subject with Rembrandt and his pupils; signed " S. Koninck." " Ft. A°. 1641." From the Boursault and Saltmarshe Collections. In the privately printed Catalogue of the latter Gallery, sold by Auction in 1846, it is elaborately described. H. 3 ft. 11 in. W. 4 ft. 5 in.

## PHILIP DE KONINGH.

B at Amsterdam 1619   D. 1689.

View in Holland, on the sea coast, a Windmill in the foreground, with Corn Fields and Figures, &c.   From the Collection of Colonel Bourgeois at Paris.   Oval.   On Panel. H. 2 ft. ½ in.   W. 2 ft. 5 in.

## H. LANCASTER.

London.

Dutch Market Boat.   From the Exhibition of the Society of British Artists, 1847, No. 124.   H. 2 ft. 4½ in.   W. 3 ft. 1½ in.

## NICHOLAS LANCRET.

B. at Paris 1690   D. there 1743.

The Arbour on the Lake, with Figures and Swans.   H. 2 ft. 11 in.   W. 2 ft. 8 in.

## PROSPER HENRY LANCRINCK.

B. at Antwerp 1628   D. in London 1692.

Landscape with Figures.   From the Collection of James Gibbs, Esq.   H. 4 ft. 7 in.   W. 5 ft. 6 in.

## LANDI.

Colossal Head of St. John.   From the Collection of Sir Simon Clarke, Bart.   H. 3 ft. 8 in.   W. 3 ft. 2 in.

## G. BRYANT LANE.

Rome.

Copy of La Bella di Tiziano in the Pitti Palace at Florence.   Imported from Rome, 1845.   H. 4 ft. 10 in.   W. 3 ft. 8 in.

Portrait of Beriah Botfield, in the uniform of a Deputy Lieutenant, taken at Rome, November, 1845. H. 4 ft. 3 in. W. 3 ft. 3 in.

## GIOVANNI LANFRANCO.
### B. at Parma 1581.   D at Rome 1647.

Head of St. Joseph. From the Gallery of Cardinal Fesch at Rome, 1845. H. 3 ft. 4 in. W. 2 ft. 10 in.

Head of an Apostle. From the Collection of Cardinal Fesch at Rome, 1845. H. 2 ft. 8 in. W. 2 ft. 4½ in.

## NICHOLAS DE LARGILLIERE.
### B. at Paris 1656.   D there 1746

Portrait of Madame Osorio de Vilasco. Engraved by Joan. Vanderbruggen, 1682. Imported from Paris. H. 5 ft. 9. W. 4 ft. 9 in.

Portrait of Mary Queen of England. Imported from Paris. H. 5 ft. 9 in. W. 4 ft. 9 in.

Portrait of M. A. Frizon de Blamont, Marquise de Fortia. "Peint par N. D. Largilliere, 1726," as recorded in the Inscription at the back. Imported from France. H. 5 ft. 9 in. W. 4 ft. 9 in.

## JULES LAURE.
### Paris 1848.

Portrait of Saint Geneviève in the habit of La Fileuse; signed "Jules Laure." Purchased in Paris, February, 1848. H. 3 ft. 3 in. W. 2 ft. 10 in.

## SIR PETER LELY.

B. at Soest in 1617    D at London 1680.

Portrait of the Countess of Suffolk.   H. 4 ft. 4 in.   W. 3 ft. 8 in.

Portrait of the Duchess of Grafton.   H. 1 ft. 9½ in.   W. 1 ft. 4½ in.

Portrait of Lady Margaret Cecil, Countess of Ranelagh. H. 1 ft. 9½ in.   W. 1 ft. 4½ in.

Portrait of Mrs. Middleton.   H. 4 ft. 9 in.   W. 4 ft.

## JOHN LINGELBACH.

B. at Frankfort 1625.   D. at Amsterdam 1687.

View of the Roman Forum during the Carnival; signed and dated, 1656.   Imported from Holland.   H. 4 ft 9 in. W. 4 ft.

View of a town in Sicily during the Carnival, with Figures Masquerading.   H. 2 ft. 7 in.   W. 2 ft. 2 in.

View of a Sicilian town, with Figures variously engaged. From a Collection at Glasgow.   H. 2 ft. 7 in.   W. 2 ft. 2 in.

## HENDRICK VAN LINT.

B. at Antwerp   Fl. 1680

View of the Coliseum at Rome.   From the Collection of the Earl of Lichfield, at Lichfield House, sold in 1842.   H. 2 ft. 6 in.   W. 4 ft. 2 in.

## PIETRO LOCATELLI.

### B at Rome. Fl. 1690.

A Landscape with Figures. From the Collection of Mr. Brightwell. H. 2 ft. 7 in. W. 4 ft. 10 in.


## BERNARDINO LUINI.

### B. at Lovini. Fl. 1500-50.

The Virgin and Child, the latter holding some Cherries. From the Collection of Sir Thomas Baring. On Panel. H. 2 ft. 5 in. W. 2 ft. 2 in.


## THOMAS LUNY.

### MARINE PAINTER.

#### Teignmouth Devon.

1779. A pair of Sea Pieces. "T. L. 1779." H. 1 ft. W. 10½ in.

1820. Mount Edgecumbe. H. 1 ft. 7½ in. W. 1 ft 11½ in.

1826. A Breeze at Sea. H. 1 ft. 3½ in. W. 1 ft. 6½ in.

1826. Men of War in a Calm. H. 1 ft. 3½ in. W. 1 ft. 6½ in.

1826. View of the River Teign. H. 1 ft. 3½ in. W. 1 ft. 6 in.

1826. Vessels Becalmed. H. 1 ft. 3½ in. W. 1 ft. 6 in.

1827. Storm off the Coast of Devon. H. 2 ft 4 in. W. 2 ft. 11 in.

1827. New Astley Brig entering Teignmouth Harbour, Dec. 1819. H. 1 ft. 6 in. W. 1 ft. 10 in.

1827. Port Royal, Jamaica; Vessels coming out of Kingston Harbour with the land breeze. H. 1 ft. 6 in. W. 1 ft. 10 in.

1827. A Seventy-four coming to Anchor in Torbay. H. 1 ft. 6 in. W. 1 ft. 10 in.

1827. Entrance of Teignmouth Harbour by Moonlight. H. 1 ft. 6 in. W. 1 ft. 10 in.

1828. The Beach at Deal. H. 1 ft. 4 in. W. 1 ft. 7½ in.

1828. Race of Portland. H. 1 ft. 7½ in. W. 1 ft. 11½ in.

1829. Yarmouth Roads. H. 3 ft. 11 in. W. 5 ft. 4 in.

1829. Asgill Force. Wensley Dale. H. 1 ft. 3½ in. W. 1 ft. 6¼ in.

1829. Fowey Harbour. H. 1 ft. 7½ in. W. 1 ft. 11½ in.

1829. Holy Island. H. 1 ft. 10¼ in. W. 2 ft. 3½ in.

[1829.] Helvoetsluys. H. 1 ft. 10½ in. W. 2 ft. 3½ in.

1830. The Caledonia and Boyne chasing the Romulus into Toulon. H. 3 ft. 11 in. W. 5 ft. 4 in.

1830. Rock of Gibraltar. H. 2 ft. 3½ in. W. 2 ft. 10 in.

1830. St. Sannazar Tower, Bay of Naples. H. 2 ft. 3½ in. W. 2 ft. 10 in.

1830. Dover Harbour. H. 1 ft. 7½ in. W. 1 ft. 11½ in.

1830. Vessels Becalmed. H. 1 ft. 4 in. W. 1 ft. 7½ in.

1830. Chase to Windward. H. 1 ft. 10½ in. W. 2 ft. 3½ in.

1830. Scarborough. H. 1 ft. 10½ in. W. 2 ft. 3½ in.

1830. Ramsgate Pier. H. 1 ft. 10½ in. W. 2 ft. 3½ in.

1830. Walmer Castle, South Foreland. H. 1 ft. 10½ in. W. 2 ft. 3½ in.

1831. Sea Cliffs, Coast of Kent. H. 1 ft. 3¼in. W. 1 ft. 6 in.

[1831.] Waterloo Bridge. H. 1 ft. 1½ in. W. 1 ft. 5 in.

1832. The Battle of the Nile. H. 3 ft. 11 in. W. 5 ft. 4 in.

1832. Portland Island. H. 3 ft. 11 in. W. 5 ft. 4 in.

1832. Shipwreck. H. 1 ft. 1¾ in. W. 1 ft. 7¼ in.

1832. Pier head. H. 1 ft. 6 in. W. 1 ft. 10 in.

1833. The Downs. H. 2 ft. 1½ in. W. 3 ft. 6 in.

1833. Cork Harbour. H. 2 ft. 1½ in. W. 3 ft. 6 in.

1833. Ilfracombe. H. 1 ft. 6 in. W. 1 ft. 10 in.

1833. Dartmouth by Moonlight. H. 1 ft. 2 in. W. 1 ft. 4 in.

1833. Storm at Sea. H. 1 ft. 4 in. W. 1 ft. $7\frac{1}{4}$ in.

1833. Fishermen landing. H. 1 ft. 4 in. W. 1 ft. 7 in.

1833. Constance. H. 1 ft. $6\frac{1}{4}$ in. W. 1 ft. $4\frac{1}{4}$ in.

1833. Fort Rouge, Calais. H. 1 ft $6\frac{1}{4}$ in. W. 1 ft. $4\frac{1}{4}$ in.

1833. Gravesend. H. 1 ft. $2\frac{1}{2}$ in. W. 1 ft. $4\frac{1}{4}$ in.

[1833.] Exmouth. H. 1 ft. 4 in. W. 1 ft. $7\frac{1}{4}$ in.

1834. Clovelly. H. 1 ft. 4 in. W. 1 ft. 7 in.

1834. Lord Exmouth's Action with the Droits des Hommes. H. 3 ft. 6 in. W. 4 ft. 8 in.

Of the forty-four pictures by this pleasing painter many were painted to orders, having frequently visited his Studio, pleasantly situated on the banks of the Teign looking upon the Ness Cliff; the others were selected from his other works there exhibited during visits paid at different times to the Coast of Devon.

## CAVALIERE BENEDETTO LUTI.

### B. at Florence 1666. D at Rome 1724.

Madonna and Bambino. Obtained from the Collection of M. Petit Bourgogne at Marseilles, 1843. H. 2 ft. $7\frac{1}{2}$ in. W. 2 ft. 4 in.

## J. MADDOX.
### London.

Portrait of a Roman Maiden at her devotions, taken at Rome, 1843. H. 2 ft. 4 in. W. 1 ft. 10½ in.

## CARLO MARATTI.
### B. at Camurano 1625. D at Rome 1713.

Head of the Virgin. From Mr. Hindley of Salford. H. 2 ft. 11 in. W. 2 ft. 8 in.

Allegorical design of the Initiation of a Monk, inscribed on a book, "AUSCULTA PRECEPTA O FILI MAGISTRI." From the Collection of Sir John Pringle. H. 4 ft. 2 in. W. 3 ft. 6 in.

The Virgin with the Infant Jesus and St. John; St. Cecilia with a harp leans over a music book, which the infant St. John holds open. From the Collection of the Earl of Coventry at Coventry House. H. 5 ft. 5 in. W. 4 ft. 8 in.

Holy Family, with the Virgin, Infants Jesus and St John, in the background St. Joseph, and St. Cecilia with a harp. From the Collection of the Earl of Coventry in London, 1844. H. 5 ft. 5 in. W. 4 ft 8 in.

Holy Family, with the Virgin, Infant Jesus and St. Joseph; a Riposo in a Landscape, after the manner of Albano. H. 3 ft. 4 in. W. 2 ft. 7 in.

## ONORIO MARINARI.
### B 1627. D. 1715.

St. Agnes, with a Lamb. Imported from Florence. H. 3 ft. 3 in. W. 2 ft. 9 in.

## HENRY MARTENS.

### London.

Representation of the Manœuvres of the South Salopian Yeomanry Cavalry, under the command of the Earl of Powis, K. G., reviewed by Major the Hon. J. Campbell Scarlett, on the Race Course at Shrewsbury, May 12, 1845. H. 3 ft. 7 in. W. 4 ft. 2 in.

Portrait of Beriah Botfield in the full uniform of the South Salopian Yeomanry Cavalry, on his charger Pilot, caparisoned for the field; taken at Shrewsbury, May 10, 1845. H. 2 ft. 3 in. W. 2 ft.

## ANTONIO RAFFAELLE MENGS.

### B at Auszig 1728. D at Madrid 1779.

The Virgin watching over the sleeping Child. From the Collection of Sir Felix Agar. H. 3 ft. 7 in. W. 4 ft. 5 in.

## GABRIEL METZU.

### B at Leyden 1615. D. there 1658.

Hagar and Ishmael; signed " G. Metzu." From the Collection of Mr. Barnard. H. 4 ft. 9 in. W. 3 ft. 11 in.

## ANTHONY FRANCIS VANDER MEULEN.

### B. at Brussels 1634. D. at Paris 1690.

The passage of a River; Louis XIV., and his staff in the foreground giving orders. From the Collection of Mr. Stewart. H. 4 ft. 3 in. W. 3 ft. 3 in.

A Reconnoitering party of Louis XIV. and his Staff, before a town in the Low Countries. From the Collection of Baron Buckmann at Ghent, 1847. H. 3 ft. 7½ in. W. 4 ft. 2½ in.

## J. GOODSALL MIDDLETON.

### London.

Portrait of William Withering, Esq., in the uniform of the Warwickshire Militia, from a drawing by Miss Elizabeth Stewart taken from life in 1808.   H. 3 ft. 2 in.   W. 2 ft. 10 in.

Portrait of Beriah Botfield, Esq., in the uniform of the South Salopian Yeomanry Cavalry, taken from life in 1844.   H. 3 ft. 2 in.   W. 2 ft. 10 in.

Portrait of Beriah Botfield, Esq., in the uniform of a Deputy-Lieutenant of Northamptonshire, with a Deer-Hound, and a view of the North Front of Norton Hall in that county, taken in 1846.   H. 4 ft. 2 in.   W. 3 ft. 6 in.

Scene from Gil Blas, where Laura introduces him to her mistress Arsenia.   H. 6 ft.   W. 5 ft. 2 in.

Portrait of Julia.   H. 5 ft. 2 in.   W. 4 ft. 5 in.

Cephalus and Procris, after Sir Joshua Reynolds.   H. 3 ft. 11 in.   W. 3 ft. 2 in.

Venus and Cupid.   H. 2 ft. 6 in.   W. 2 ft. 11 in.

Portrait of the Artist himself when in Italy.   H. 3 ft. 11 in.   W. 3 ft. 2 in.

Portrait of a Lady in a Greek dress, 1843.   H. 3 ft. 11 in.   W. 3 ft. 3 in.

Portrait of an Italian Peasant; " La Preghiera."   H. 3 ft. 11 in.   W. 3 ft. 3 in.

Portrait of Beriah Botfield, after Miniature by Engleheart, æt. 42, 1810.   H. 3 ft. 2 in.   W. 2 ft. 10 in.

Portrait of Beriah Botfield, his son, æt. 35, 1842.   H. 3 ft. 2 in.   W. 2 ft. 10 in.

Portrait of Charlotte Botfield, after Miniature by Engleheart, æt. 32, 1810.   H. 3 ft. 2 in.   W. 2 ft. 10 in.

Portrait of Thomas Botfield, æt. 62, 1814, after sketch in Crayons by George Sharpler.   H. 3 ft. 2 in.   W. 2 ft. 10 in.

Portrait of William Botfield, æt. 58, 1814, after sketch in Crayons by George Sharpler.   H. 3 ft. 2 in.   W. 2 ft. 10 in.

Portrait of Beriah Botfield in his Study at Norton Hall, æt. 36, 1843.   H. 4 ft. 2 in.   W. 3 ft. 6 in.

## PIERRE MIGNARD.

### B 1610 at Troyes   D. 1695 at Paris.

Portrait of Prince Charles Edward Stuart.   H. 5 ft. 3 in. W. 4 ft. 4 in.

## MICHAEL JANSEN MIREVELT.

### B at Delft 1568.   D. there 1641.

Portrait of Prince Maurice of Nassau, K. G.   H. 3 ft. 1 in. W. 2 ft. 8 in.

Portrait of Francis Lord Bacon, æt. 52, date 1620; signed. H. 4 ft. 8 in.   W. 3 ft. 8 in.

Portrait of the wife of Francis Lord Bacon, æt. 42, date 1620; signed. Imported from Holland, 1844. On Panel. H. 4 ft. 8 in. W. 3 ft. 8 in.

## PIETRO FRANCESCO MOLA.

B at Lugano 1609   D. at Venice, 1665.

The Flight into Egypt. From the Collection of the Baroness de Rothschild. H. 2 ft. 7 in. W. 3 ft.

## JODOCUS MOMPERT.

B 1580   D. 1638

View on the Rhine, with distant hills, and Figures, &c. H. 2 ft. 10. W. 2 ft. 2 in.

View of a Village, in the Rhine Country, with Figures, &c. H. 2 ft. 10 in. W. 2 ft. 2 in.

Imported from Holland. On Panel.

## B. MONAMI.

Rome

View of the Forum Romanum and the Capitol at Rome; signed " B. Monami, Roma, 1845." H. 2 ft. 1 in. W. 2 ft. 8 in.

View of the Arches of Constantine and Titus, and other Ruins, seen from the Colosseum; signed " B. Monami, Roma, 1844." H. 2 ft. 1 in. W. 2 ft. 8 in.

## GEORGE MORLAND.

B 1763 in London.   D in London 1806.

The Smugglers. Obtained from G. H. Morland, Esq., the Nephew of the Artist. H. 3 ft. 4 in. W. 4 ft. 1 in.

D

## FREDERICK MOUCHERON.

### B. at Embden 1633.   D. at Amsterdam 1686

Landscape with Figures; signed and dated, 1675. Imported from Paris.   H. 3 ft. 3 in.   W. 3 ft. 11 in.


## FREDERICK MOUCHERON.

## JOHN LINGELBACH.

### B. at Frankfort 1625.   D at Amsterdam 1687.

Apennine Landscape, a Mountain stream spanned by a wooden bridge. The Figures by John Lingelbach ; signed " Moucheron, ft." From the Cabinet of Baron Buckmann of Ghent.   H. 3 ft. 7½ in.   W. 4 ft. 3½ in.


## PIEDRO DE MOYA.

### B. in Spain 1610.   D at Granada 1666.

The Virgin and Child. From the Collection of W. Ellis, Esq. H. 6 ft.   W. 5 ft. 2 in.


## C. L. MULLER.

### Paris 1844.

Carilda, une dame Espagnol qui attend un Rendezvous; signed " C. L. Muller."   H. 5 ft.   W. 4 ft.


## PATRICK NASMYTH.

### B. at Edinburgh 1787.   D in London 1831.

1824. View near West Hoathly, Sussex. From the Collection of W. S. Bond, Esq.   H. 3 ft. 1 in.   W. 3 ft. 8 in.

## PETER NEEFS.

B. at Antwerp 1570.  D. 1651.

## F. FRANCKS.

B 1580.  D 1642.

Interior of the Cathedral at Antwerp; signed " Peter Neefs, 1648." The Figures by F. Francks; signed by him. On Panel.  H. 2 ft. 6 in.  W. 2 ft. 11 in.

Interior of a Flemish Church.  The Figures by F. Francks; signed " Peeter Neefs." From the Collection of Count Bernardi, Procureur du Roi Charles X. at Bordeaux.  On Panel.  H. 2 ft. 6½ in.  W. 1 ft. 11½ in.

View of the Interior of the Cathedral at Antwerp; signed " Peter Neefs, 1648." The Figures by F. Francks, with his signature " Fr. Francks." From the Collection of Mr. Lushington, 1845.  On Panel.  H. 2 ft. 6 in.  W. 2 ft. 11 in.

## ARNOLD VAN DER NEER.

B. at Amsterdam 1619   D. 1683

View of a Fortified Town, Windmill and Ruins by Moonlight; with the Monogram of the Painter.  On Panel.  H. 2 ft. 1 in.  W. 2 ft. 7 in.

## EGLON HENDRICK VAN DER NEER.

B at Amsterdam 1643.  D. 1703

An Officer of the Arquebusiers with his Matchlock, standing with the Guard in a street at Utrecht, the Church tower is seen in the back ground.  From the Collection of Colonel Bourgeois at Paris, 1845.  H. 1 ft. 11 in.  W. 1 ft. 8 in.

## SUOR PLAUTILLA NELLI.

### A Florentine Lady d. 1588, æt 65.

The Holy Family. This artist acquired her skill in paint-ing solely from the study of some designs of FRA BARTO-LOMEO, which she had in her possession. She became a Dominican Nun of St. Catherine at Florence. From the Collection of the Duke of Lucca, acquired by H. R. H. from a Convent. On Wood. H. 3 ft. 11 in. W. 3 ft. 2 in.

## GASPARD NETSCHER.

### B. at Prague 1636. D. at the Hague 1684.

Portrait of a Lady in White Satin, walking in a Flower Garden; signed " G. Netscher, fecit," with date of 1681. Imported from France. H. 3 ft. 8 in. W. 3 ft.

A Boy blowing bubbles at a table, on which are a Chalice, a Candlestick, &c. and a rich cloth. From the Collection of Monsieur le Comte d'Harcourt at Paris, 1846. H. 1 ft. 9 in. W. 1 ft. 6 in.

Portrait of the Earl of Clarendon in his robes as Lord Chancellor of England. From the Collection of the Baroness de Rothschild. H. 2 ft 6 in. W. 2 ft. 3 in.

Portrait of a Lady seated at a table, on which stands a Vase with a Bouquet of Flowers. Purchased at Christie's. H. 2 ft. 4 in. W. 2 ft.

## JOHN NEWBOLT.

### Rome.

View of the Lake and Town of Nemi, in the Alban Hills; signed " J. Newbolt, Rome, 1845." H. 2 ft. 5 in. W. 3 ft. 1½ in.

View of the Parco di Colonna, below Marino, between Frascati and Castel Gandolfo, on the Alban Hills; signed " J. Newbolt, Rome, 1845." H. 2 ft. 5 in. W. 3 ft. 1½ in.

View of Ostia at the Mouth of the Tiber; signed " J. Newbolt, Rome, 1846. H. 1 ft. 10 in. W. 1 ft. 4 in.

View of the Town of Riana, in the Sabine Hills; signed " J. Newbolt, Rome, 1846." H. 1 ft. 10 in. W. 1 ft. 4 in.

View of the Castle of St. Angelo and St. Peters at Rome, taken from the banks of the Tiber; signed " J. Newbolt, Rome, 1845." H. 2 ft. 5 in. W. 3 ft. 1½ in.

View of the Ponte Rotto, the Temple of Vesta and Church of St. Maria in the Cosmedin, from the opposite bank of the Tiber; signed " J. Newbolt, Rome, 1844." H. 2 ft. 5 in. W. 3 ft. 1½ in.

View of the Claudian Aqueduct, on the Campagna, with Rome in the distance; signed " J. Newbolt, Rome, 1845." H. 2 ft. 5 in. W. 3 ft. 1½ in.

View of the Torre de tre teste on the Campagna, the Alban Hills in the background; " signed " J. Newbolt, Rome, 1845." H. 2 ft. 5 in. W. 3 ft. 1½ in.

View of Roma Vecchia, and the Alban Hills. H. 1 ft. 3 in. W. 11 in.

View of the Grotto of Egeria and Temple of Bacchus. H. 1 ft. 3 in. W. 11 in.

View of the Tomb of Cecilia Metella. H. 1 ft. 3 in. W. 11 in.

View of the Tomb of Accius Plautius on the Ponte Lucano, with Adrian's Villa, 1844. H. 1 ft. 3 in. W. 11 in.

View of Ostia at the Mouth of the Tiber. H. 2 ft. 8 in. W. 2 ft. 2 in.

View of Riana on the Sabine Hills, 1846. H. 2 ft. 8 in. W. 2 ft. 2 in.

## JOSEPH FRANCIS NOLLEKENS.
### B. at Antwerp 1706. D. in London 1748.

Interior of the Saloon at Wanstead House, with an assemblage of Ladies and Gentlemen at a Concert or Converzazione, among whom are portraits of Lord and Lady Tilney. From the Collection of Mr. Long Wellesley Pole, at Wanstead House, sold June 20th, 1822. Cat. p. 121, No. 318, for £127 1s. On Copper. Mounted on Panel. H. 2 ft. 3 in. W. 2 ft. 9 in.

## JAMES NORTHCOTE.
### B at Devonport 1746   D in London 1831.

Portrait of William Pitt, in his robes as Chancellor of the Exchequer. H. 3 ft. 7 in. W. 3 ft.

## OCCIALI.
### Verona.

View of Lombardy, from the left bank of the Adige; signed and dated " Gasparo Witel, 1714." From the Collection of Sir Simon Clarke, Bart. H. 2 ft. 8 in. W. 4 ft. 4 in.

View of Naples. Strada di S. Lucia, and Pizzofalcone.
H. 2 ft. 2 in. W. 3 ft. 4 in.

## J. B. OMMEGANCK.
### B. at Antwerp  D 1826

Landscape in Guelderland, with Cattle and Figures; signed
" J. B. Ommeganck." Imported from Paris, 1844. H.
2 ft. 4½ in. W. 2 ft. 10 in.

## JOHN OPIE.
### B at Truro 1761.  D in London 1807.

The Gipsy. From the Collection of the Earl of Coventry
in London, 1844. H. 3 ft. 5 in. W. 3 ft.

The Schoolmistress. H. 4 ft. W. 3 ft. 1 in.

## B. VAN ORTH.
### Mayence.

Assumption of the Virgin; a reduced copy of the Picture by
Guido in the Munich Gallery. Purchased at Mayence in the
Exposition of 1842, from the Artist himself. On Wood.
H. 2 ft. 7½ in. W. 2 ft.

## ALESSANDRO VAROTARI, IL PADUANINO.
### B. at Padua 1590.  D. at Venice 1650.

Mater Dolorosa. Imported from Spain. H. 5 ft. 4 in.
W. 4 ft. 8 in.

## ANTHONY STAEVERTS PALAMEDES.
### B. at Delft 1601.  D. 1680.

Interior with a Musical Party. H. 1 ft. 8 in. W. 1 ft.
11 in.

## GIACOMO PALMA, IL VECCHIO.

### B. at Serinalta 1540-8. D 1596-1623

The Holy Family. From the Collection of M. Petit Bourgogne at Marseilles. H. 1 ft. 11 in W. 2 ft. 2 in.

## DOMENICO PANETTI.

### B at Ferrara 1460. D 1530.

The Death of the Virgin, with the eleven Apostles. From the Collection of Count Barba at Ferrara. On Panel. H. 6 ft. 8 in. W. 7 ft. 7 in.

This Picture was exhibited at the British Institution in June 1848, and elicited the following remark from the Athenæum of June 17. "The *Death of the Virgin*, by Domenico Panetti (102), ought not to be overlooked:—the student will find in it much to reward his attention. The actions are natural and fine : - they imply dignity of person and sympathy with the scene. The heads are highly expressive and full of variety,—the colour is rich and skilfully contrasted,—and the draperies are well disposed. The whole is a very useful picture for the artist's contemplation. As a specimen of Ferrarese art it is one of the best for the purpose."

## CAVALIERE GIOVANNI PAOLO PANINI.

### B at Piacenza 1691. D. at Rome 1758.

Interior of the Pantheon at Rome. From the Collection of the Earl of Lichfield at Shugborough Hall. Cat. 1842. H. 5 ft. 3 in W. 4 ft. 4 in.

Landscape with Figures and Ruins at Rome. From the Collection of Richard Bayley, Esq., Castle Dyke, near Sheffield. H. 3 ft. 6 in. W. 4 ft. 5 in.

## WILLIAM PARROTT.

General View of the Forum of Pompeii; painted from the Triumphal Arch. It is considered the most perfect specimen of the ancient Forum extant; it was excavated between the years 1813 and 1822. It had suffered from the earthquake of the year 63, and at the period of the fatal eruption sixteen years after was being reconstructed with great magnificence. The Forum was the most public place of resort in Pompeii, around it are the remains of its once sumptuous Temples, it Treasury, its Law Tribunals, its Colleges, &c. Stone measures fitted into a recess in the wall of the area indicate the market-place of this commercial city of Campania; signed " W. Parrott, Pompeii, 1845." The Copyright of the Picture is reserved by the Artist.   H. 2 ft. 4 in.   W. 3 ft. 8⅝ in.

## PIETRO VANUCCI, IL PERUGINO.
### B. at Perugia 1446.   D at Florence 1524.

The Holy Family.   On Panel.   H. 3 ft. 5 in.   W. 2 ft. 8 in.

The Virgin, with glory, in a blue mantle with a star, embracing the Infant Jesus, seated on a crimson cushion. From the Palazzo Ricardi at Florence, 1848.   On Panel.   H. 2 ft. W. 1 ft. 2½ in.

## THOMAS PHILLIPS.
### London.   D. 1844.

Portrait of the Rev. William Buckland, D.D., Professor of Geology in the University of Oxford, subsequently Dean of Westminster, taken in 1830.   H. 4 ft. ¾ in.   W. 3 ft. 3 in.

Portrait of Beriah Botfield, Esq , with Norton Hall in the distance, taken in 1828, aged 21. H. 7 ft. 10 in. W. 4 ft. 9½ in.

## SEBASTIAN DEL PIOMBO.
### B. at Venice 1485. D. at Rome 1547.

Portrait of Alonzo Cano. From the Collection of Richard Bayley, Esq., Castle Dyke near Sheffield. On Panel. Oval. H. 3 ft. 3 in. W. 2 ft. 6 in.

## CORNELIUS POELEMBURG.
### B. at Utrecht 1586. D. there 1660

Landscape with Figures. On Panel. H. 1 ft. 10 in. W. 1 ft. 8 in.

The Adoration of the Magi. From the Collection of William Beckford, Esq. late of Fonthill. H. 2 ft. 1 in. W. 1 ft. 10 in.

## FRANCIS PORBUS, THE YOUNGER.
### B at Antwerp 1570. D. at Paris 1622

Portrait of the Pensionary Jean de Witte. Engraved from the Collection of Sir Frederick Roe, Bart. H. 3 ft. 1½ in. W. 2 ft. 8 in.

## PAUL POTTER.
### B. at Enkhuysen 1625. D. 1654

A Herdsman and Cattle. Called the Young Bull. "Paulus Potter, 1647," a reduced copy, made in 1815, from the large Picture in the Museum at the Hague. From the Collection of the Earl of Coventry. H. 2 ft. 4 in. W. 2 ft. 11 in.

## GASPAR POUSSIN.

### B. at Rome 1613  D there 1675.

Landscape on a River, with a view of a Convent near Tivoli. From the Collection of Monsieur Ferriere Laffitte at Paris, 1846. H. 2 ft. W. 2 ft. 4 in.

A Landscape composed of the scenery of the Grotta Ferrata in the Alban Hills near Rome. From the Cabinet of Monsieur le Comte Michel at Paris, 1846. H. 1 ft. 10½ in W. 2 ft. 5 in.

Landscape with Figures. H. 3 ft. 3 in. W. 2 ft. 9 in.

Landscape with Figures H. 3 ft. 3 in. W. 2 ft. 9 in.

## J. PRINS.

### Holland c. 1670

View of the Church and Town of Haerlem, with Figures. From the Collection of J. Stewart, Esq., 1847. H. 2 ft. 3 in. W. 2 ft. 8 in.

## EDWARD PRITCHETT.

### London

View of the Town Hall at Leipsic. Exhibited at the British Institution, 1846, Cat. No. 113. H. 3 ft. 2 in. W. 2 ft. 7 in.

## DOMENICO PULIGO.

### B at Florence 1475.  D. there 1527.

The Virgin and Infant Jesus. From the Collection of the Baroness de Rothschild. H. 5 ft. 1 in. W. 4 ft. 1 in.

## MADAME PULINI.

The Interview between Cardinal de Richelieu and Marie de Rohan after Decaisné; signed "M<sup>me</sup> Pulini, 1840." On China. H. 1 ft. 9 in. W. 1 ft. 6½ in.

## ADAM PYNAKER.

### B at Pynaker near Delft 1621. D. 1673

Landscape with Figures; signed " A. Pynaker." Imported from Holland. H. 4 ft. 1 in. W. 3 ft. 6 in.

## RAFFAELLO SANZIO.

### B March 28, 1483 D. April 7, 1520.

La Bella Fornarina; from the original in the Florence Gallery, copied by ANNA TEERLINK in 1844. H. 3 ft. 1½ in. W. 2 ft. 5 in.

## RAUH.

### Rome

Portrait of a Roman Lady and her child; signed " Rauh, Roma, 1837." Obtained from the Artist. H. 4 ft. 2 in. W. 3 ft. 4 in.

## SEBASTIANO RICCI.

### B at Belluno 1659 D. at Venice 1734.

Christ at Emmaus. The penitent Magdalen at the feet of the Saviour. From the Collection of the Viscountess Hampden. H. 2 ft. 8 in. W. 3 ft. 7 in.

## DOMENICO RICCIO.

### B at Verona 1494. D at Venice 1567

The Holy Family. From the Collection of Wynne Ellis, Esq. H. 8 ft. 4 in. W. 6 ft. 2 in.

The Holy Family. A Friar and Nun of the order of St. Dominic adoring. From the Collection of the Baroness de Rothschild. W. 7 ft. 3 in. W. 6 ft.

## HYACINTHE RIGAUD.
### B at Perpignan 1663. D at Paris 1743

Portrait of Madlle. de Blois, Fille de Louis XIV. et Madame de la Valliere, Princesse de Conti. Inscribed on the back " fait par Hyacinthe Rigaud, 1701." Imported from Paris, 1837. H. 5 ft. 9 in. W. 4 ft. 9 in.

## J. ROBERTS.

View of the Doge's Palace, and Prisons at Venice. On Panel. H. 2 ft. 1 in. W. 1 ft. 10 in.

## GIOVANNI FRANCESCO ROMANELLI.
### B at Viterbo 1617 D there 1662.

Holy Family; the Virgin and Child with St. Joseph. From the Gallery of Bishop Luscombe at Paris, December, 1846. H. 6 ft. W. 5 ft.

## GIULIO PIPPI ROMANO.
### B. at Rome 1492. D. at Mantua 1546.

The Virgin and Child surrounded by Angels, with a Vase, &c. Imported from Italy. On Panel. H. 4 ft. W. 3 ft. 5 in.

## THEODORE ROMBOUTS.
### B at Antwerp 1597. D there 1637.

Landscape, a Cottage by a pool, on which is a white duck, and a boat, with Figures. With the Monogram of the Painter. From the Collection of General Rutter at Amsterdam, 1847. On Panel. H. 2 ft. 2 in. W. 2 ft. 8 in.

## WILLIAM VAN ROMEYN.

### Holland c 1665.

Landscape with Cattle and Figures; signed " W. Romeyn ft." From the Collection of Count Bernardi at Bordeaux. H. 1 ft. 11 in. W. 2 ft. 2 in.

## GEORGE ROMNEY.

### B at Dalton 1734    D. there 1802.

Portrait of Lady Hamilton, as a Shepherdess. H. 3 ft. 3 in. W. 2 ft. 10 in.

## JACOB RUYSDAEL.

### B. at Haerlem 1636    D there 1681.

View of Scheeveling; signed "J. R." Imported from Holland. H. 4 ft. 9 in. W. 6 ft. 5 in.

## SOLOMON RUYSDAEL.

### B at Haerlem 1616.   D. there 1670

View of Haerlem; signed "S. Ruysdael." From the Collection of Sir Felix Agar. H. 2 ft. 8 in. W. 3 ft. 6 in.

Duck Shooting. Obtained from Leyden. H. 2 ft. 10 in. W. 3 ft. 11 in.

Landscape with Figures. From the Collection of Mr. Mills. H. 4 ft. 6 in. W. 6 ft. 6 in.

View of Haerlem; signed " S. Ruisdael, 1645." From the Collection of Colonel Braddyll at Ulverstone Priory, 1846. H. 4 ft. 6 in. W. 6 ft. 1 in.

## GIOVANNI BAPTISTA SALVI, IL SASSOFERRATO.

B at Sassoferrato near Urbino 1605    D. at Rome 1685

The Virgin and Child.    From the Collection of M. Petit Bourgogne at Marseilles.    On Panel.    H. 2 ft. 6 in.    W. 2 ft. 2 in.

## ANDREA VANUCCHI, DEL SARTO.

B at Florence 1488    D. 1530.

The Virgin and St. John, upon whom the Infant Christ is in the act of bestowing his blessing.    From the Collection of M. Coesvelt, sold in 1837.    The large fresco of this subject is in a Convent near Sienna.    On Panel.    H. 2 ft. 9 in. W. 2 ft. 3 in.

## IPPOLITO SCARSELLA, LO SCARSELLINO.

B at Ferrara 1560    D. 1621.

The Madonna and Bambino    From the Casa Tanari at Ferrara co-eval with the painter's life.    Purchased from G. Bryant Lane at Rome in 1845, who bought it from a dealer in pictures at Ferrara.    H. 3 ft.    W. 2 ft. 6 in.

## WILLIAM SCHELLINCKS.

B. at Amsterdam 1632    D 1678

Interior of a Study, with a Philosopher seated at a table, surrounded by books and papers; signed " W. Schellincks." Imported from Holland    H. 2 ft. 6 in.    W. 2 ft. 5 in.

## BARTOLOMMEO SCHIDONI.

B at Modena 1560.    D there 1616

The Virgin and Child.    From the Collections of Mr. Gray of Haringay, and Mr. Johnson of Manchester.    H. 3 ft. 3 in. W. 2 ft. 8 in.

## M. SCHOEVAERDTS.

### A native of Flanders. Fl. 1700.

Landscape with Figures; signed " M. Schoevaerdts," and dated 1700. On Panel. H. 1 ft. 11 in. W. 2 ft. 6 in.

View of a Flemish Town, with Figures. From the Collection of the Baroness de Rothschild. On Panel. H. 1 ft. 11 in. W. 2 ft. 6 in.

## G. SERRITELLI. ·

### Naples.

View of the Temples of Pæstum on the Gulf of Salerno, taken in 1845 ; signed " G. Serritelli." From the Artist at Naples. H. 2 ft. 4 in. W. 3 ft.

## ELISABETTA SIRANI.

### B at Bologna 1638    D 1664.

Nymph burning the Arrows of Love. Imported from Florence. H. 2 ft. 11½ in. W. 2 ft. 6 in.

The Immaculate Conception. From the Collection of Count Celestine at Florence, in whose family it had remained for more than a hundred years. Exhibited at the British Institution, 1845. H. 5 ft. 2 in. W. 4 ft. 2 in.

## PETER VAN SLINGELANDT.

### B at Leyden 1640. D 1691.

Interior of a House in Holland, the Master seated at a table with a pipe in one hand and a jug in the other, the wife leans over the back of the chair, while a man seated opposite plays on the violin, the nurse and two children are looking in at the door, a dog on the floor. From the Collection of the Chevalier Cousin at Paris. Exhibited at the British Institution, 1847. On Panel. H. 2 ft. 1 in. W. 1 ft. 10 in.

Interior of a Dutch Gentleman's Mansion, the Master seated at a covered table, which is approached by his wife and daughter, the Pug dog seated on the floor. From the Collection of the Duc de Richelieu at Paris, 1848. On Panel. H. 1 ft. 11 in. W. 2 ft. 4 in.

## ANTONIO SOLARIO.
### B at Abruzzo. D at Naples c. 1455.

The Holy Family, St. Joseph presenting the Infant Jesus with a bunch of cherries. From the Collection of M. Bernardy, Procureur du Roi Charles X. at Paris. On Panel. H. 2 ft. 3 in. W. 2 ft.

## GIUSEPPE RIBERA, IL SPAGNOLETTO.
### B at Xativa 1589. D. at Naples 1656

The Piping Boy, or Itinerant Musician of Naples. H. 3 ft. 3 in. W. 2 ft. 6 in.

## JAMES STARK.
### Windsor.

View in North Wales. Obtained from the Artist. H. 2 ft. 11 in. W. 3 ft. 11 in.

A Water Mill. Exhibited at the Royal Academy in 1847, and purchased from the Artist. H. 3 ft. 1 in. W. 2 ft. 9 in.

E

## HENRY STEENWYCK.

B. at Steenwyck in Holland 1550. D. 1603

Interior of a Church during Evening Service. From the Collection of M. le Vicomte d'Harcourt at Paris. Cat. p. 19, No. 45, 1841-2. On Panel. H. 2 ft. 3 in. W. 2 ft. 11 in.

## JAMES STELLA.

B. at Lyons 1596. D. at Paris 1647.

Holy Family, with St. Joseph, and Female Saints. From the Collection of Monsieur le Comte Michel at Paris, 1846. H. 1 ft. 11. W. 1 ft. 7 in.

A Magdalen recumbent under a rock by the side of a stream, over her head are three Cherubim. From the Collection of the Earl of Errol. H. 5 ft. 2 in. W. 4 ft. 1 in.

The Holy Family, with Saint John and the Lamb, a stag, and old man with flowers; at an open window a cat is endeavouring to reach a bird in a cage; signed " J. Stella, ft. 1634." Imported from Paris, 1846. H. 2 ft. W. 1 ft. 8 in.

## HENRY STONE.

D. at London 1653.

Portrait of Sir Thomas Gresham, Founder of the Royal Exchange, with his Arms, and date, 1579. From the Collection of Colonel Braddyll at Conishead Priory, 1846. H. 3 ft. 1 in. W. 2 ft. 7½ in.

## ABRAHAM STORCK.

B at Amsterdam 1650. D. there 1708.

Dutch Vessels with Boats off the Coast, with fishermen on

the shore; signed " A. Storck, fecit." From the Collection of the Hon. Francis Charteris.   H. 2 ft. 8 in.   W. 3 ft. 1 in.

A Sea Piece.   H. 3 ft. 6 in.   W. 3 ft.

The Quay of a City.   H. 3 ft. 6 in.   W. 3 ft.
Both signed " A. Storck," and dated 1676.

## ANNA TEERLINK.
### Rome 1844.

The Peasant of Genzano; Portrait of the Mother and Child drawn from nature at Rome; signed "Anna Teerlink nata Muochi, Roma, 1844."   H. 4 ft. 2 in.   W. 3 ft. 4 in.

## DAVID TENIERS, JUN.
### B. at Antwerp 1610   D. at Brussels 1694.

A Dutch Farm Yard, with Cattle, Sheep and Figures; signed " D. Teniers, ft."   From the Collection of Baron Denon at Paris, 1846.   H. 2 ft. 2 in.   W. 2 ft. 9 in.

A Battle piece, representing a Skirmish of Cavalry on the edge of a Wood, with a Village Spire in the distance, and the signature " D. T."   From the Collection of Monsieur Casimir Perrièr at Paris, 1840.   H. 3 ft. 1 in.   W. 3 ft. 9 in.

## GERARD TERBURG.
### B. at Zwoll 1608.   D. at Deventer 1681.

Portrait of Count Propagandi, Ambassador at the Court of Spain, with a Greyhound, and some Charts on a table.   H. 3 ft. $6\frac{1}{2}$ in.   W. 3 ft. $\frac{1}{2}$ in.

Portrait of the Countess Propagandi, the lady of the Ambassador, with a Spaniel. H. 3 ft. 6½ in. W. 3 ft. ½ in.

From the Cabinet of Chevalier Cousin at Paris.


## J. B TIFFIN.
### London.

Caxton's House in the Almonry, Westminster. From the Exhibition of 1847 at the British Institution, No. 345. H. 1 ft. 3 in. W. 1 ft. 2 in.


## GIACOMO ROBUSTI, IL TINTORETTO.
### B. at Venice 1512. D. there 1594

The Miracle of St. Mark, a Bozzetto or Sketch for the great picture at Venice. From the Collection of the Duke of Lucca, 1841. Inherited by his Royal Highness from Charles IV. of Spain, his Grandfather. No. 30 in the Catalogue. H. 3 ft. 2 in. W. 3 ft. 10 in.


## TIZIANO VECELLI DA CADORE.
### B at Cadore 1480. D. at Venice 1576.

The Virgin and Child, to whom Magdalen is presenting a Vase of Incense, St. Joseph standing by; the latter being a portrait of Titian himself. Imported from Florence. On Panel. H. 2 ft. 1 in. W. 2 ft 4 in.

La Bella di Tiziano, in the Pitti Palace at Florence, copied by G. B. LANE.

Venus rising from the Sea. A Copy by an unknown Artist. H. 3 ft. 8 in. W. 3 ft. 2 in.

## LE TOCQUE.

1718. Portrait of Prince Charles Stuart. On Wood. H. 1 ft. 1 in. W. 1 ft.

## BENNO TOERMER.
### Rome 1847.

Evening at Rome; two Italian Girls in the Gardens of the Medici Villa at Rome, St. Peter's in the distance; signed " B. Toermer, Roma, 1846." H. 3 ft. W. 2 ft. 6 in.

## JOHN WALLACE TUCKER, JUN.
### Exeter.

1828. Norton Hall, East Front, in 1810. H. 1 ft. 4½ in. W. 1 ft. 7½ in.

1830. Norton Hall from the Watling Street. H. 1 ft. 3 in. W. 1 ft. 6 in.

1830. Mill Bay on the Dart. H. 2 ft. 4 in. W. 2 ft. 9½ in.

1830. Lankey Mill, North Devon. H. 1 ft. 4½ in. W. 1 ft. 6½ in.

1830. A Cottage in Devonshire. H. 1 ft. 4½ in. W. 1 ft. 6½ in.

1831. Norton Hall, South East View, 1828. H. 1 ft. 4½ in. W. 1 ft. 7½ in.

[1831.] Norton Church and Village. H. 1 ft. 4½ in. W. 1 ft. 7½ in.

1831. Norton Hall in 1801. H. 1 ft. 7 in. W. 2 ft.

1831. Norton Hall in 1828. H. 1 ft. 7 in. W. 2 ft.

1834. St. David's Church from Northernhay, Exeter. H. 1 ft. 6 in. W. 1 ft. 3 in.

[1834.] Exeter Castle. H. 1 ft. 1¼ in. W. 1 ft. ½ in.
The Views of Norton Hall by this Artist were copied from Sketches taken from nature by the late William Withering, Esq., L.L.D., and vary in some respects from the originals.

## WILLIAM TURNER.
### Oxford
View of Oxford, Christ Church Meadows, and the Isis. Painted for Beriah Botfield at Oxford in 1827-8. H. 3 ft. 2 in. W. 4 ft. 11 in.

## LUCAS VAN UDEN.
### B. at Antwerp 1595. D. 1660.
## DAVID TENIERS, JUN.
Woodland Scene on the banks of a river, with persons engaged in fishing; the figures inserted by David Teniers, jun. who has represented himself, in a red cloak, standing by the water. From the Collection of Monsieur le Comte d'Harcourt at Paris, 1846. On Copper. H. 2 ft. 11 in. W. 3 ft. 11 in.

## PIETRO BUONACORSI, PIERINO DEL VAGA.
### B near Florence 1500    D. at Rome 1547
Infant Saviour, St. John and the Virgin. From the Collection of G. Morland, Esq., who obtained it from Count Ruspoli at the Ruspoli Palace near Florence. On Wood. H. 4 ft. 5 in. W. 3 ft. 7 in.

## DIRK, or THEODORE, VALKENBURG.

### B at Amsterdam 1675.   D. there 1721

Flower piece; signed " D. Valkenburg." H. 4 ft. 1 in. W. 3 ft. 8 in.


## SIR ANTHONY VANDYCK.

### B. at Antwerp 1599.   D at London 1641.

Portrait of Margaret Lemon, his mistress, as Judith. From Horace Walpole's Collection at Strawberry Hill, who purchased it from the Collection at Buckingham House. Cat. p. 211.   H. 3 ft. 2 in.   W. 2 ft. 8 in.


Portrait of Frances Stuart, Countess of Portland, when about 26 years of age, seen in a three-quarter view, dressed in a dark silk and a light brown mantle on the shoulders, with the bodice richly decked with pearls,—the right hand is placed in front and the left holds a bunch of red roses.   From the Collection of Jeremiah Harman, Esq. Catalogue No. 86; See Smith's Catalogue, p. 135, No. 490.   H. 4 ft. 5 in. W. 3 ft. 7 in.


## PHILIP VANDYCK.

### B at Amsterdam 1680.    D. at the Hague 1752.

A Mother and Child, with Flowers and Fruit.   From the Collection of Charles Lushington, Esq.   H. 2 ft. 3 in. W. 1 ft. 10 in.


## J. VERHEYEN.

### Belgium 1847.

Interior of the Bourse at Antwerp; signed " Verheyen ft." Imported from the Artist in Holland.   H. 1 ft. 6 in. W. 1 ft. 8½ in.

## VERMEULEN.

Fl Holland 1810. D. c. 1822.

A Winter Scene on a River in Holland, with Figures skating and a Booth on the Ice; signed "Vermeulen." H. 2 ft. 9 in. W. 3 ft. 6 in.

A Wintry Landscape, a Church and distant Town in Holland; signed "Vermeulen." H. 2 ft. 9 in. W. 3 ft. 8 in.

A View on a River in Holland,—a Winter Scene, with Figures, &c. sporting on the Ice; signed "Vermeulen." H. 3 ft. 1 in. W. 4 ft. 1 in.

## JOSEPH VERNETS.

B at Avignon 1712. D. 1786.

View of a Port in the Mediterranean, with Vessels and Figures; signed "J. Vernets, 1774." Oval. H. 3 ft. 10½ in. W. 4 ft. 9 in.

## PAOLO CAGLIARI, IL VERONESE.

B. at Verona 1532. D. there 1588

The Annunciation. H. 3 ft. 9 in. W. 3 ft. 3 in.

## SIMON DE VLIEGER.

B. at Amsterdam 1612 D. there 1670.

A View on the Coast of Holland, with Shipping and Fishermen, &c.; signed "S. D. V. 1649." Imported from Holland. On Panel. H. 2 ft. 5 in. W. 3 ft. 1 in.

## ANTHONY WATTEAU.

B. at Valenciennes, 1684.   D. at Paris 1721.

A Pastoral Scene with Figures.   From Mr. Johnson of Manchester.   H. 2 ft. 5 in.   W. 2 ft. 10 in.


## G. WEBSTER.

Man of War off Gravesend.   H. 3 ft. 4 in.   W. 4 ft.

Tilbury Fort.   On Panel.   H. 1 ft. 8 in.   W. 2 ft. 3 in.

Gravesend.   On Panel.   H. 1 ft. 7 in.   W. 1 ft. 11 in.

Purfleet.   On Panel.   H. 1 ft. 7 in.   W. 1 ft. 11 in.

On the River.   On Panel.   H. 1 ft. $1\frac{1}{2}$ in.   W. $11\frac{1}{2}$ in.


## JOHN BAPTIST WEENINX.

B. at Amsterdam 1621.   D. 1660.

View of a ruined Temple, and a Convent, with Figures; probably a view in the Levant.   From the Collection of Chevalier Cousin at Paris, 1846.   H. 2 ft. 5 in.   W. 3 ft.

The Water Party, a scene in the Levant, with a White Swan on the water, and a flight of steps from a landing place, whence a Boat is putting off.   From the Collection of Chevalier Cousin at Paris, 1845.   H. 2 ft. $2\frac{1}{2}$ in.   W. 2 ft. 9 in.


## THEODORE WELLER.

Rome

The Hermit of Terracina, distributing alms.   He is presenting a Portrait of Pius IX. to a child, forming part of a group of Italian Contadini, assembled near Terracina; signed " Theodor Weller, Rome, 1848." H. 3 ft. 2 in. W. 3 ft. 8 in.

## WILLIAM E. WEST.

### Pisa

Portrait of Lord Byron. H. 3 ft. 8 in. W. 3 ft. 2 in.

Portrait of Teresa Guiccioli, with her Autograph Signature at the back, 1822. H. 3 ft. 8 in. W. 3 ft. 2 in.

These Portraits were taken from Nature at Pisa in 1822. A duplicate of the first by the same artist is in the possession of Joseph Neeld, Esq. The present came from the Collection of William Joy, Esq. for whom they were painted.

## PENRY WILLIAMS.

### Rome.

Morning at Rome; two Roman women with their children, the tower of Santa Croce and the Aqueducts, as seen from the Colosseum, in the distance; signed " Penry Williams, Roma, 1848." H. 3 ft. W. 2 ft. 6 in.

The Goatherd of the Campagna, with his dog and flock; the Claudian Aqueduct in the distance; signed " Penry Williams, Rome, 1846." H. 1 ft. 6 in. W. 1 ft. 3 in.

The Roman Maiden, engaged in Spinning; signed " Penry Williams, Rome, 1845." H. 1 ft. 6 in. W. 1 ft. 3 in.

## EMANUEL DE WITTE.

### B. at Alkmaer 1607 D at Haerlem 1692.

Interior of a Church in Holland, with Figures; with the

date 1685; signed. From the Collection of J. Stewart, Esq. H. 3 ft. 1 in. W. 2 ft. 9 in.

Interior of a Catholic Church in Holland; signed "E. de Witte," and dated 1652. On Panel. Imported from Holland. H. 2 ft. 5 in. W. 2 ft. 1 in.

The Interior of a Church in Holland; with Figures, &c. signed and dated 1661. Imported from Holland. H. 2 ft. 6 in. W. 2 ft.

The Interior of a Dutch Church, with Figures. Imported from Holland. H. 2 ft. W. 1 ft. 9 in.

## PETER WOUVERMANS.

### B. at Haerlem 1625. D. 1683.

Entrance of a Stable Yard, with Horses and Figures; signed "P. W." From the Collection of M. Petit Bourgogne at Marseilles. H. 2 ft. W. 2 ft. 3 in.

## JOHN WYNANTS.

### B. at Haerlem 1600. D. 1670.

## JOHN LINGELBACH.

A Landscape representing a country road, with Figures inserted by John Lingelbach; some hills in the distance; signed "J. Wynants, 1650." From the Collection of Chevalier Cousin at Paris, 1845. H. 1 ft. 10 in. W. 2 ft. 2½ in.

A View of the Park at the Hague, shewing the entrance to that Town, with Figures introduced by John Lingelbach; signed "J. Wynants, 1650." From the Collection of Monsieur le Comte d'Harcourt at Paris, 1846. H. 3 ft. 8 in. W. 3 ft. 3 in.

## HENDRICK MARTENS ZORGH.
### B. at Rotterdam 1621  D. 1682.

Interior, with a Family Party of Hollanders at a Festive Board; signed " M. Zorgh, 1644." Imported from Belgium. H. 2 ft. 2 in. W. 2 ft. 8 in.

## FRANCESCO ZUCCARELLI.
### B. at Florence 1710.  D there 1788.

Italian Landscape, with Peasants at a Fountain, and a Boy driving Cows and Sheep. From the Collection of Mr. Archbutt. H. 2 ft. 7 in. W. 3 ft. 7½ in.

Bacchanalian Scene, with Fauns and Nymphs dancing. H. 1 ft. 6 in. W. 1 ft. 10½ in.

Pastoral Scene ; Shepherds and Shepherdesses reposing. H. 1 ft. 6 in. W. 1 ft. 10½ in.

A Classical Landscape, with Figures. Italian scenery. H. 3 ft. W. 4 ft. 2 in.

## FEDERIGO ZUCCHERO.
### B. in Italy 1543.  D. at Ancona 1609

Portrait of Queen Katherine Parr, wife of Henry VIII. From P. Huggett, Esq. of Sandgate. H. 4 ft. 6 in. W. 3 ft. 6 in.

Portrait of Queen Elizabeth. From P. Huggett, Esq. of Sandgate. H. 4 ft. 9 in. W. 3 ft. 10 in.

Portrait of Sir Francis Walsingham, with a View of his House at Scadbury in Kent. From the Collection of Sir Robert Walpole, and subsequently in that of Horace Walpole. Sold at Strawberry Hill, May 18, 1842. Engraved in Houbraken's Heads. H. 4 ft. 6 in. W. 3 ft. 7 in.

Portrait of Mary Queen of Scots, of early date. From P. Huggett, Esq. of Sandgate. On Panel. H. 2 ft. 4 in. W. 2 ft.

### FRANCESCO ZURBARAN.
B. near Seville 1596    D at Madrid 1662.

The Assumption of the Virgin. From the Collection of Mr. Gee at Manchester. H. 6 ft. 5 in. W. 5 ft. 1 in

---

## ANONYMOUS.

Portrait of Sir William Dugdale, the Warwickshire Antiquary. H. 3 ft. 9 in. W. 3 ft. 5 in.

Portrait of a Warwickshire Gentleman, in a blue dress. H. 4 ft. 7 in. W. 3 ft. 8 in.

The Companion, probably his brother, both family Portraits, from a Mansion in Warwickshire. H. 4 ft. 7 in. W. 3 ft. 8 in.

Portrait of William Ingilby, Parliamentary General during the Civil Wars. H. 5 ft. W. 3 ft. 10 in.

Portrait of an old Man, " æt. 82," with the date of " 1639." H. 3 ft. 3 in. W. 2 ft. 10 in.

Portrait of Prince Charles Stuart. Purchased at Edinburgh from Mr. Forest in 1829. H. 2 ft. 4 in. W. 2 ft.

Portrait of Henry Rich, Earl of Holland, beheaded by the Rebels, March 9th, 1648-9. Oval. H. 2 ft. 2 in. W. 1 ft. 10 in.

Portraits of his Daughters. H. 2 ft. 2 in. W. 1 ft. 10 in.

Portrait of John Milton, æt. 35, Aº 1643. From the Collection of Horace Walpole at Strawberry Hill, 1842. Cat. p. 207. H. 4 ft. 4 in. W. 3 ft. 7 in.

Portrait of King Henry VII., at his Devotions; of early date. On Panel. H. 5 ft. W. 3 ft. 3 in.

Portrait of King Edward VI., probably contemporaneous. On Panel. H. 4 ft. 8 in. W. 3 ft. 8 in.

Portrait of Lady Jane Grey. H. 5 ft. W. 4 ft.

Portrait of King Charles II. H. 4 ft. 9 in. W. 4 ft.

Portrait of the Earl of Pembroke. H. 5 ft. 2 in. W. 4 ft. 6 in.

Portrait of Dutch Burgomaster, with a pen. H. 3 ft. 7 in. W. 2 ft. 11 in.

Portrait of Dutch Burgomaster, the companion. H. 3 ft. 4 in. W. 2 ft. 8 in.

Portrait of Lady Coventry.   H. 5 ft. 2 in.   W. 4 ft. 6 in.

Portrait of Lady —— Coventry.   H. 5 ft. 2 in.   W. 4 ft. 6 in.

Belle, a Spaniel.   H. 10½ in.   W. 1 ft. ½ in.

Pincher, a Terrier.   H. 10½ in.   W. 1 ft. ½ in.
      Favourite Dogs of Beriah Botfield at Oxford.

Hare and dead Game.   H. 10 in.   W. 8½ in.

Pheasant and dead Game.   H. 10 in.   W. 8½ in.

Fox in Cover.   H. 8½ in.   W. 11¾ in.

City by Moonlight.   On Copper.   H. 11 in.   W. 1 ft. 1¼ in.

View near the Devil's Bridge, South Wales.   H. 1 ft. 2 in.   W. 1 ft. 4 in.

Village by Moonlight.   On Wood.   H. 1 ft.   W. 1 ft. 3 in.

The Gipsy Camp.   H. 1 ft. 4 in.   W. 1 ft. 9 in.

# WATER-COLOUR DRAWINGS.

### WILLIAM BISHTON.

Venus and Cupid, after Correggio in the National Gallery.
H. 1 ft. 9 in. W. 1 ft. 6 in.

### GEORGE BROWN.

1825. Head of Christ. H. 1 ft. 4 in. W. 1 ft. 2 in.

The Loves of the Angels. H. 1 ft. 8 in. W. 1 ft. 6 in.

1827. The Torch of Love. H. 1 ft. 6½ in. W. 1 ft. 4 in.

Innocence. H. 1 ft. 6 in. W. 1 ft. 8 in.

The Bird's Nest. H. 1 ft. 6 in. W. 1 ft. 8 in.

Venus and Cupid. H. 1 ft. 1½ in. W. 1 ft. 3 in.

Rebecca in Ivanhoe. H. 1 ft. 4 in. W. 1 ft. 2¼ in.

Miss Chester, as Beatrice in Much Ado about Nothing. H. 1 ft. 5 in. W. 1 ft. 2½ in.

La Contessa Teresa Guiccioli. H. 1 ft. 5½ in. W. 1 ft. 3 in.

1827.  The Lily of the Valley.  In Morocco Case.  H. 6½ in.
W. 8 in.

Awaking, after Westall.  In Morocco Case.  H. 6½ in.
W. 8 in.

1831.  Titian's Venus.  In Morocco Case.  H. 7¼ in.
W. 5½ in.

## J. BUCKLER.

The Monument of Cyril Jackson, Dean of Christ Church,
by Chantrey, in Christ Church Cathedral.  H. 2 ft. 9 in.
W. 2 ft. 6½ in.

## ALFRED EDWARD CHALON, R. A.
### London.

Portrait of Beriah Botfield, Esq., æt. 22, taken in 1830.
In a Gold Locket.

Portrait of Julia, with John o' Groat, a Skye-Terrier, taken
in 1830.  In a Frame and Rosewood Case.  H. 1 ft. 4½ in.
W. 11½ in.

Portrait of Julia, taken in 1830.  In a Gold Locket.

## SAMUEL COX.
### Daventry

View of Norton from the New Orchard.  H. 9⅝ in.  W. 1 ft.
3 in.

View of Norton Hall in 1801.  H. 7 in.  W. 10½ in.

F

View of Norton Hall in 1811. H. 7 in. W. 10½ in.
Both from the New Orchard.

View of Norton Hall in 1801. H. 10½ in. W. 1 ft 2 in.

View of Norton Hall in 1828. H. 1 ft. 1½ in. W. 1 ft. 6½ in.

## SAMUEL COX, JUN.
### Daventry.
View of the Entrance Hall at Norton Hall, 1842. Engraved.

## GILLESPIE.

1821. Portrait of Beriah Botfield, æt. 14, August 1821.
In Profile. H. 5¼ in W. 4¼ in.

John Wynne Griffith, Esq. of Garn, Co. Denbigh.
In Profile H. 5¼ in. W. 4¼ in.
The Profile likenesses were taken by an itinerant Artist at Daventry.

## HARDING.

Venus and Cupid. H. 6 in. W. 4½ in.

## CHARLES LANDSEER.
### London
The Temptation of St. Anthony. In a Frame and Rosewood Case. H. 1 ft. 2½ in. W. 1 ft.

## WILLIAM JOHN NEWTON.

Portrait of Beriah Botfield, æt. 21, 1828. In Morocco Case.

Portrait of Beriah Botfield, æt. 23, 1830. Engraved. H. 1 ft. 3 in. W. 1 ft. 2 in.

## HENRY PERRY.
### London.

Carisbrooke Castle Gateway. H. 10 in. W. 1 ft. ¼ in.

## FANNY RAY, now LEVETT.

1820. St. Boniface, Undercliff, Isle of Wight. H. 7¼ in. W. 10 in.

1820. Binstead Parsonage, near Ryde, Isle of Wight. H. 8 in. W. 11 in.

View of Symond's Yat on the Wye. H. 1 ft. 10 in. W. 2 ft. 3¾ in.

Landscape, a Composition. H. 1 ft. 8 in. W. 2 ft. 3½ in.

View of St. Leonard's on the Sea. H. 1 ft. 6½ in. W. 2 ft. 4 in.

## F. ROCHARD.
### London.

Le Mantelet Noir. Obtained from the Artist, 1848.

## SOPHIA SAUNDERS.

### Cheltenham.

1824.  Diana with the Bow.  H. 1 ft. 1¾ in.  W. 1 ft. ½ in.

Louisa Venoni.  H. 1 ft. 1 in.  W. 1 ft.

Flora Mac Ivor.  H. 1 ft. ½ in.  W. 11½ in.

1828.  Diana Vernon.  H. 1 ft. 1½ in.  W. 1 ft. ½ in.

The Sleepers.  In Morocco Case.  H. 6 in.  W. 8½ in.

The Countess of Morton.  H. 10½ in.  W. 9½ in.

1829.  Portrait of Lady Peel, after Sir Thomas Lawrence, P. R. A.  H. 1 ft. 1½ in.  W. 1 ft. ½ in.

Hawking.  H. 1 ft. 1½ in.  W. 1 ft. ½ in.

Thorn in the foot.  H. 1 ft. 1½ in.  W. 1 ft. ½ in.

1830.  Timbolene, or the Castanets.  H. 1 ft. 2 in.  W. 1 ft. 1 in.

Venus Aphrodite.  H. 1 ft. 1½ in.  W. 1 ft. ½ in.

Albanian Girl.  H. 1 ft. 1½ in.  W. 1 ft. ¼ in.

Pomona.  In Morocco Case.  H. 7 in.  W. 9 in.

1831  Titian's Daughter.  H. 1 ft. 1½ in.  W. 1 ft.

1831.　La Huerfana de Leon, after Henry Liverseege. See the Winter Wreath for 1831, pp. 181-192. H. 1 ft. 1¾ in　W. 1 ft. ½ in

L' Odalisque.　In Rosewood Case.　H. 1 ft. ½ in. W. 1 ft. 4 in.

1832.　The Light of the Harem.　In Rosewood Case　H. 1 ft. ½ in.　W. 1 ft. 4 in.

The Widow, after Rochard.　See the Talisman for 1831, p. 198, and Le Keepsake Français 1831, pp. 148-163.　H. 10½ in.　W. 9½ in.

Juliet, after Miss Sharpe　See the Keepsake of 1831, pp. 18-39.　H. 10¾ in.　W. 10 in.

Haidee, after C. L. Eastlake, R.A　See the Frontispiece to the Keepsake of 1831, pp 216-18. H. 10¾ in.　W. 10 in.

[1833.]　Bouquet d'Amour.　In Rosewood Case.　H. 1 ft. 2 in　W. 1 ft. 5 in.

1834.　The Rose without a Thorn.　In Rosewood Case. H. 1 ft. 6 in.　W. 1 ft. 8 in.

### ELISABETH STEWART.

Portrait of William Withering Esq. in the Uniform of the Warwickshire Militia, taken in 1808, aged 32.

### JOHN WALLACE TUCKER, JUN.
#### Exeter.
The Promenade.　H. 1 ft. 5 in.　W. 1 ft. 2 in.

The Soirée. H. 1 ft. 5 in. W. 1 ft. 2 in.

## WILLIAM TURNER.

View of Blenheim Palace, Oxon. H. 1 ft. 6 in. W. 2 ft. 1 in.

View of Magdalen Church Bridge, Oxford. Obtained from the Artist at Oxford, 1828. H. 1 ft. 4 in. W. 1 ft. 8¼ in.

Diana Venatrix, Blenheim. H. 1 ft. 2¾ in. W. 1 ft. ½ in.

## WILLIAMS.

St. Anthon's Well, Holyrood. H. 1 ft. 3½ in. W. 1 ft. 8 in.

Edinburgh, from Calton Hill. H. 1 ft. 3½ in. W. 1 ft. 8 in.

## WILLIAM WITHERING, LLD.

A Franciscan Friar at his Devotions. H. 2 ft. 3 in. W. 1 ft. 9½ in.

## WOODDEROOFFE.

Bitton Church Yard, Tomb of Mrs. Ellicombe. H. 1 ft. W. 1 ft. 3 in.

Bitton Vicarage, in pencil. H. 11 in. W. 1 ft. 2 in.

# ANONYMOUS.

Mary Queen of Scots.   H. 1 ft. ½ in.   W. 11 in.

Le Repos.   In Morocco Case.   H. 7 in.   W. 8½ in.

Queen of Paphos.   In Morocco Case.   II. 9 in.   W. 7 in.

The Necklace.   H. 9¾ in.   W. 9 in.

Portrait of Madame Vestris.   H. 1 ft. 1 in.   W. 11¼ in.

# CRAYON DRAWINGS.

### GEORGE SHARPLES.

Portrait of Beriah Botfield, after Miniature by Engleheart, 1814. H. 1 ft. 3 in. W. 1 ft. 2 in.

Portrait of Charlotte Botfield, his wife, with her son Beriah Botfield, æt. 7, 1814. H. 1 ft 3 in. W. 1 ft. 2 in.

Portrait of Lydia, wife of William Withering, Esq. of the Larches, [1814]. H. 1 ft. 3 in. W. 1 ft. 2 in.

Portrait of Charlotte Botfield, aged 35, and her son Beriah Botfield, aged 7, 1814. H. 1 ft. 3 in. W. 1 ft. 2 in.

Portrait of William Withering, Esq. of the Larches, aged 38, 1814. H. 1 ft. 3 in. W. 1 ft. 2 in.

# MINIATURES.

## WILLIAM BOOTH.

### Died 1845

#### PUPIL OF SIR WILLIAM ROSS, R. A.

Miss Kitty Fisher, as " Cleopatra dissolving the Pearl," copied from the original Picture by Sir Joshua Reynolds H. $8\frac{1}{2}$ in.   W. $7\frac{1}{2}$ in.

Charles I. after Vandyck.

Henri Quatre.

Napoleon.

Anne of Austria.

La Fontaine.

Mary Queen of Scots.

## DAVID ENGLEHEART.

### London

Beriah Botfield, Esq. of Norton Hall, B. July 27, 1768. M. July 26, 1806.   D. April 27, 1813.   H. $2\frac{3}{8}$ in.   W. $2\frac{1}{8}$ in.

Charlotte Botfield, wife of the above.   B. Feb. 21, 1778. M. July 26, 1806.   D. Oct. 26, 1825.   H. $2\frac{1}{2}$ in. W. 2 in.

Beriah Botfield, son of the above, taken Sept. 1808, aged 1 year and 6 months. H. 2½ in. W. 1½ in.

William Withering, M.D., after a Portrait by C. von Breda. B. March 28, 1741. D. Oct. 6, 1799. H. 2⅞ in. W. 2⅜ in.

William Withering, LLD., son of the above, taken in 1808. B. Nov. 21, 1776. M. Aug. 8, 1808. D. June 23, 1832. H. 2⅞ in. W. 2¼ in.

## JOHN PETITOT.

B. at Geneva 1607. D. at Veray 1691.

Portrait of Louis XIV. when advanced in life. From the Collection of George IV. in a Tortoise-shell Snuff Box.

Portrait of Philip V. of Spain. From the Collection of George IV. in a Tortoise-shell Snuff Box.

Portrait of the Great Condé, in a Tortoise-shell Snuff Box.

## CHRISTIAN FREDERIC ZINCKE.

B at Dresden 1684 D. at London 1767.

Portrait of Ethelreda Harrison, the wife of Charles Viscount Townsend, after a picture by JOHN BAPTIST VANLOO, B. at Aix 1684, D. there 1746. In a richly enamelled frame, with her Arms supported by Cupids, enamelled by Groth, on the reverse. From the Collection of Horace Walpole, at Strawberry Hill, engraved for the new Edition of his Letters. Cat. p. 142.

# ADDENDA.

## THOMAS DESSOULAVY.

### Rome.

General View of Rome, from the Villa Freeborn on the opposite bank of the Tiber; signed "T. Dessoulavy, Rome, 1846." H. 2 ft. 8 in. W. 3 ft. 6 in.

General View of Naples from the hill of Posilippo; signed "T. Dessoulavy, Rome, 1846." H. 2 ft. 8 in. W. 3 ft. 6 in.

View of the Colosseum at Rome from the Convent of S. Gregorio; signed "T. Dessoulavy, Rome, 1846." H. 2 ft. 8 in. W. 3 ft. 6 in.

View of the Ruins of the Palace of the Cæsars at Rome; signed "T. Dessoulavy, Rome, 1846." H. 2 ft. 8 in. W. 3 ft. 6 in.

View of the Cascatelli, and the Villa of Mecænas at Tivoli, from the opposite bank of the Anio; signed "T. Dessoulavy, Rome, 1846." H. 2 ft. 8 in. W. 3 ft. 6 in.

View of Lunghezza on the Campagna of Rome; signed "T. Dessoulavy, Rome, 1846." H 2 ft. 8 in. W. 3 ft. 6 in.

———

## ERRATA.

Page 5, line 1, *for* Blaar *read* Blaas.

   13, — 10, *for* Bonyl *read* Borough.

   21, — 4, *read* H. 3 ft. 3 in.   W. 4 ft. 8 in.

   28, — 14, *for* orders *read* order.

   32, — 8 and 11, *for* Sharpler, *read* Sharples.

   34, — 18, *for* Carilda *read* Casilda.

   51, — 10, *for* Muochi, *read* Muschi.

   67, — 21, *add* H 1 ft. 5 in. W. 1 ft. 2 in.

At p. 29, the third and fourth articles describe the same picture by Carlo Maratti.

The second and third articles in p. 37, occur again in p. 38.

# INDEX OF NAMES.

| | PAGE | | PAGE |
|---|---|---|---|
| Aglio, A. | 1 | Bourdon, Sebastian | 8 |
| Antonissen | ib | Brakenburg, Rainier | ib. |
| Anonymous | 61-63 70 | Brooking, C. | 9 |
| Artois, Jacques D' | 2 | Brown, George | 64 |
| Asch, Peter John Van | ib | Buckler, J. | 65 |
| Asselyn, John | ib | | |
| | | Calvert, F. | 9 |
| Bahtia, Giacomo | ib | Cangeza | ib. |
| Baroccio, Federigo | ib. | Caracci, Annibale | ib |
| Bassano, Il, Giacomo da Ponte | 3 | Caracci, Antonio, Il Gobbo | ib |
| Bassi, J. | ib. | Caravaggio, Michel Angelo Ame- | |
| Begeyn, Abraham | ib. | rigi da | 10 |
| Bennett, William | ib | Castiglione, Giovanni Benedetto | ib. |
| Berghem, Nicholas | 4 | Cavedone, Giacomo | ib. |
| Berkheyden, Gerard | ib. | Chalon, A Edward, R.A. | 65 |
| Bishton, William | 64 | Cigoli, Ludovico Cardi | 10 |
| Boddington, Henry John | 4 | Clint, Alfred | ib. |
| Blaar, Charles | 5 | Coleman, Charles | 11 |
| Bloemen, J. F. Orizzonte | ib | Condé, Lieutenant | 12 |
| Bloot, Peter | ib | Correggio, Antonio Allegri | ib. |
| Bodeman, J. | ib | Correggio, Pomponio Allegri | ib. |
| Boilly | ib | Cox, Samuel | 12, 65 |
| Bol, Ferdinand | 6 | Cox, Samuel, jun. | 66 |
| Bonifazio Veneziano | ib. | Cunliffe, Daniel | 13 |
| Booth, William | 73 | | |
| Borgognone, Il, J. Courtois | 6 | | |
| Both, John | 6, 7 | Davison, Jeremiah | ib |
| Boucher, Francis | 7 | Dawe, George | ib |
| Boultbee, J. | ib | Decker, Francis | 14 |

| | PAGE | | PAGE |
|---|---|---|---|
| Dessoulavy . . . | 3 | Janssens, Abraham . . . . | 20 |
| Diepenbeck, Abraham Van | 14 | Joli, Antonio . . . . . | 21 |
| Dietrich, C. William Ernest | ib | | |
| Dolci, Agnese . . . . . . ib. | | | |
| Dolci, Carlo . . . . | 15 | Kearsley, Harriet . . . . . . ib. | |
| Domenichino, Domenico Zam- | | Keisar, William de . . . . ib. | |
| pieri . . . . . . ib. | | Kneller, Sir Godfrey . . . . ib. | |
| Duc, John Le . . . . ib. | | Koninck, Solomon . . . ib. | |
| | | Koningh, Philip de . . . 22 | |
| | | | |
| Eeckhout, Gerbrant Vander . ib. | | | |
| Engleheart, David . . . | 73 | Lancaster, H. . . . . . ib. | |
| Everdingen, Aldret Van . . . | 15 | Lancret, Nicholas . . . . . . ib. | |
| | | Lancrinck, Prosper Henry . . ib. | |
| | | Landi . . . . . . . . ib. | |
| Franck, John Baptist . . . ib. | | Landseer, Charles . . . . | 66 |
| Franks, Frederick . . . . 16, 35 | | Lane, G. Bryant . . . . . | 22 |
| | | Lanfranco, Giovanni . . . . | 23 |
| | | Largilliere, Nicholas de . . ib. | |
| Gainsborough, Thomas . | 16 | Laure, Jules . . . . . . ib. | |
| Garofalo, Benvenuto Tisio . ib | | Lely, Sir Peter, . . . | 24 |
| Gillespie . . . . . . | 66 | Lingelbach, John . 17, 24, 34, 59 | |
| Giordano, Luca . . . . | 16 | Lint, Hendrick Van . . 24 | |
| Glover, John . . . . . . | 17 | Locatelli, Pietro . . . . . | 25 |
| Goyen, John Van . . . . . | ib | Luini, Bernardino . . . . . . ib. | |
| | | Luny, Thomas . | 25-28 |
| | | Luti, Cavaliere Benedetto . . | 28 |
| Hackaert, John . . . ib | | | |
| Hannemann, Adrian . . . 18 | | | |
| Harding . . . . | 66 | Maddox, J. . . . | 29 |
| Harp, Gerard Van . . . . . | 18 | Maratti, Carlo . . . . . ib | |
| Helst, Bartholomew Vander . ib | | Marinari, Onorio . . . . ib. | |
| Hofland, T. C . . . . | 19 | Martens, Henry . . 30 | |
| Hogarth, William . . . ib. | | Mengs, Antonio Raffaelle . ib | |
| Holme . . . . . . . . ib. | | Metzu, Gabriel . . . . ib | |
| Hornbrook, T. L. . . . . . ib. | | Meulen, A. F. Vander . . ib. | |
| Huysum, John Van . . . . ib. | | Middleton, J Goodsall . . 31 | |
| | | Mignard, Pierre . . . . | 32 |
| | | Mirevelt, Michael Jansen . ib | |
| Janssen, Cornelius . . . . | 20 | Mola, Pietro Francesco . . | 33 |

| | PAGE | | PAGE |
|---|---|---|---|
| Mompert, Jodocus . . | 33 | Poussin, Gaspar . . . . | 43 |
| Monami, B. . . . | ib. | Prins, J . . . | ib. |
| Morland, George . . | ib | Pritchett, Edward . . . . | ib. |
| Moucheron, Frederick . | 34 | Puligo, Domenico . | ib. |
| Moya, Piedro de . . . . . | ib. | Pulini, Madame . . . . . | 44 |
| Muller, C L. . | ib. | Pynaker, Adam . . . . . | ib. |
| | | | |
| Nasmyth, Patrick . . | ib | Raffaello Sanzio . . . . | ib. |
| Neefs, Peter . . . . . . | 35 | Rauh . . . . . . . . . | ib. |
| Neer, Arnold Vander . . | ib | Ray, Fanny, now Levett . . | 67 |
| Neer, Eglon Hendrick Vander | ib. | Ricci, Sebastiano - . . . | 44 |
| Nelli, Suor Plautilla . . . . | 36 | Riccio, Domenico . . . | ib. |
| Netscher, Gaspard . . . | ib | Rigaud, Hyacinthe . . | 45 |
| Newbolt, John . . . . . | ib. | Roberts, J. . . . . . . | ib |
| Newton, William John . . . | 67 | Rochard, F. . . . | 67 |
| Nollekens, Joseph Francis . | 33 | Romanelli, Giovanni Francesco | 45 |
| Northcote, James . . | ib | Romano, Giulio Pippi . | ib. |
| | | Rombouts, Theodore . . . . | ib. |
| | | Romeyn, William Van . . | 46 |
| Occiali . . . . . . . | ib | Romney, George . . . | ib. |
| Ommeganck, J. B . . . | 39 | Ruysdael, Jacob . . . . | ib |
| Opie, John . . . . . . . | ib. | Ruysdael, Solomon . . . . | ib |
| Orth, B. Van . | ib. | |
| | | Sassoferrato, Il, Giovanni Bap- | |
| Paduanino, Il, Aless. Varotari . | ib. | tista Salvi . . . . . . . | 47 |
| Palamedes, Anthony Staeverts | ib. | Sarto, Andrea Vanucchi del . | ib |
| Palma, Giacomo, Il Vecchio . | 40 | Saunders, Sophia . . . | 68 |
| Panetti, Domenico . . . . | ib. | Scarsellino, Lo, Ippolito Scar- | |
| Panini, Cavaliere Giovanni Paolo | ib. | sella . . . . | 47 |
| Parrott, William . . . . . | 41 | Schellincks, William . . . . | ib. |
| Perugino, Il, Pietro Vanucci . | ib. | Schidoni, Bartolommeo . . . | ib. |
| Perry, Henry . . . . . . | 67 | Schoevaerdts, M. . . . . . | 48 |
| Petitot, John . . . . . . | 74 | Serritelli, G. . . . . . . | ib. |
| Phillips, Thomas . . . . | 41 | Sharples, George . . . . . | 72 |
| Piombo, Sebastian del . . . | 42 | Sirani, Elisabetta . . . . . | 48 |
| Poelemberg, Cornelius . . . | ib | Slingelandt, Peter Van . . . | ib. |
| Porbus, Francis, the Younger | ib. | Solario, Antonio . . | 49 |
| Potter, Paul . . . . | ib. | Spagnoletto, Il, Giuseppe Ribera | ib. |

| | PAGE | | PAGE |
|---|---|---|---|
| Stark, James | 49 | Vandyck, Philip | 55 |
| Steenwyck, Henry | 50 | Vanloo, John Baptist | 74 |
| Stella, James | ib. | Verheyen, J. | 55 |
| Stewart, Elisabeth | 69 | Vermeulen | 56 |
| Stone, Henry | 50 | Vernets, Joseph | ib. |
| Storck, Abraham | ib. | Veronese, Il, Paolo Cagliari | ib |
| Stothard, T. | 1 | Vlieger, Simon de | ib. |
| | | | |
| Teerlinck, Anna | 51 | Watteau, Anthony | 57 |
| Teniers, David, Jun | 2, 51, 54 | Webster, G | ib. |
| Terburg, Gerard | 51 | Weeninx, John Baptist | ib. |
| Tiffin, J B | 52 | Weller, Theodore | ib. |
| Tintoretto, Il, Giacomo Robusti | ib. | West, William E. | 58 |
| Tiziano Vecelli da Cadore | ib | Williams, Penry | ib |
| Tocque, Le | 53 | Williams | 70 |
| Toermer, Benno | ib | Withering, William, LLD. | ib |
| Tucker, John Wallace, Jun. | 53, 69 | Witte, Emanuel De | 58 |
| Turner, William | 54, 69 | Woodderooffe | 70 |
| | | Wouvermans, Peter | 59 |
| | | Wynants, John | ib. |
| Uden, Lucas Van | 54 | | |
| | | Zincke, Christian Frederic | 74 |
| | | Zorgh, Hendrick Martins | 60 |
| Vaga, del, Pietro Buonacorsi Pierino | 54 | Zuccarelli, Francesco | ib |
| Valkenburg, Dirk, or Theodore | 55 | Zucchero, Federigo | ib. |
| Vandyck, Sir Anthony | ib. | Zurbaran, Francesco | 61 |

LONDON:
WILLIAM NICOL, SHAKSPEARE PRESS,
PALL MALL.

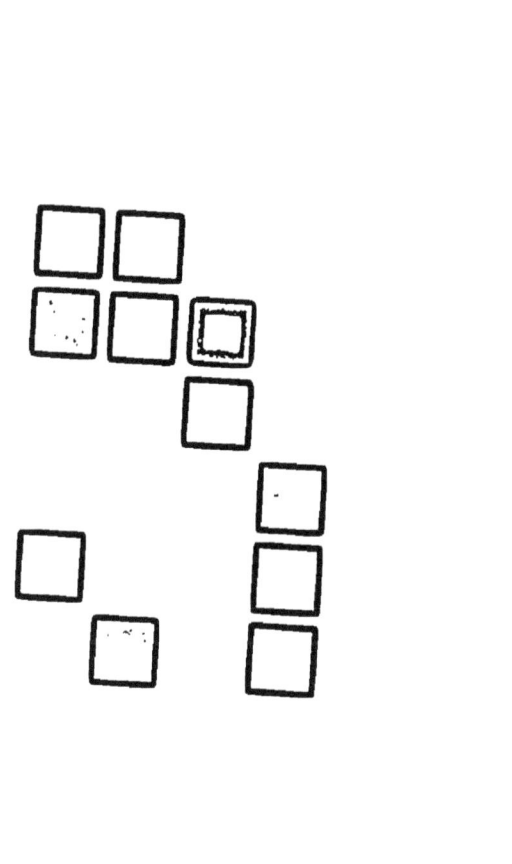

Lightning Source UK Ltd.
Milton Keynes UK
UKHW022254240720
367142UK00009B/204